Copyright © 2018 Cathrine Dahl
All rights reserved.
ISBN: 978-82-93697-19-0

- Successful Dating -

No More Frogs

Get to know the

MALES

in the zodiac

by
Cathrine Dahl

CONTENTS

Page 1 | **PREFACE: A few words about compatibility**
and why traditional compatibility guides can give you the wrong idea

Get to know your date.
Blind Date, Speedy Essentials
• The Essence • Who's waiting for you? • Emergency fixes for embarrassing pauses • Your place or mine? • Checklist

Aries	|5	Taurus	|39	Gemini	|73
Cancer	|107	Leo	|141	Virgo	|175
Libra	|209	Scorpio	|243	Sagittarius	|277
Capricorn	|311	Aquarius	|345	Pisces	|379

CHAPTER 1: Prepare Yourself
• Top 10 Attention Grabbers • His Dream Date. The Essence of her • His Arousal Meter

Aries	|9	Taurus	|43	Gemini	|77
Cancer	|111	Leo	|145	Virgo	|179
Libra	|213	Scorpio	|247	Sagittarius	|281
Capricorn	|315	Aquarius	|349	Pisces	|383

CHAPTER 2: The First Date
• Getting your foot in the door • Whatever you do, don't…
• Signs you're in – or not • Not your type? Making an exit

Aries	|13	Taurus	|47	Gemini	|81
Cancer	|115	Leo	|149	Virgo	|175
Libra	|217	Scorpio	|251	Sagittarius	|285
Capricorn	|319	Aquarius	|353	Pisces	|387

TIP: Be a little creative about it. Coming up with something new, even if it's just a detail, will make you stand out. Thinking outside the box is fine - however, don't toss the box away!

CHAPTER 3: Sex'n Stuff
• How to get him in the mood • Preferences and erotic nature
• Hitting the right buttons • His expectations • His vs. your erotic preferences

Aries		19	Taurus		53	Gemini		87
Cancer		121	Leo		155	Virgo		189
Libra		223	Scorpio		257	Sagittarius		291
Capricorn		325	Aquarius		359	Pisces		393

CHAPTER 4: The Big Picture
• His personality - Pros and Cons • Romantic vibes • Erotic vibrations

Aries		25	Taurus		59	Gemini		93
Cancer		127	Leo		161	Virgo		195
Libra		229	Scorpio		263	Sagittarius		297
Capricorn		331	Aquarius		365	Pisces		399

CHAPTER 5: Compatibility Quiz

Aries		31	Taurus		65	Gemini		99
Cancer		133	Leo		167	Virgo		201
Libra		235	Scorpio		269	Sagittarius		303
Capricorn		337	Aquarius		371	Pisces		405

- Successful Dating -
No More Frogs

by Cathrine Dahl

No More Frogs - Successful Dating is your one-stop dating guide. No unnecessary blah-blah. The information is right here, at your fingertips.

This guide can be used in several ways. It's a handy tool when you want to prepare yourself a little. It can give you an advantage when going on a date or getting to know someone you've just met - or even someone you've known for a while.

Although this guide can help you angle your approach, remember to be true to yourself. Have fun, be wise, follow your heart - and keep your feet on the ground!

- Cathrine Dahl

Preface:
A few words about compatibility, and why compatibility guides can give you the wrong idea.

So you've met this Gemini you really, really like, but you're a Scorpio, and the compatibility guides say you're a lousy match. Guess what? That's rubbish!

Some compatibility guides offer a very simplistic approach, claiming that your best matches are the star signs within the same element as you:

Fire: Aries, Leo and Sagittarius
Earth: Taurus, Virgo and Capricorn
Air: Gemini, Libra and Aquarius
Water: Cancer, Scorpio and Pisces

Other guides are slightly more specific, declaring that we are compatible with star signs within our astrological polarity.

Yin: Taurus, Virgo, Capricorn, Cancer, Scorpio and Pisces
Yang: Aries, Leo, Sagittarius, Gemini, Libra and Aquarius

Doesn't look too good, does it? The most optimistic approach has removed half of the population from your dating pool. It doesn't make any sense. The true picture is far more promising...

One star sign, two very different personalities

Each of us has a unique astrological thumbprint determined by the sun, the moon and the planets. The most important factors being your ascending star (ascendant), the sun (star sign) and the moon (feelings).

Let's make it simple
Imagine your star sign being a melody. All the other aspects (the unique positioning of the moon and the planets) are sound effects, applied by a producer with a mixer.

The combination of rhythm, depth and base creates your unique sound. Another person with the same star sign will get his own sound mix and end up with a different beat.

Your personal melody can create wonderful harmonies with star signs you're not supposed to get on with – and nothing but noise with signs that are meant to be matches. You won't find out until you get to know each other.

Let's get to know your date…

ARIES the male

YOUR DATE: ARIES
21 March–20 April

The Essence of him

Restless – dynamic – aggressive – impulsive – makes things happen – has a boyish charm; can be slightly childish – energetic – jealous – generous – absent-minded – kind – temperamental – clever – social – has a good sense of humour – confident – passionate – determined – a creative lover – disorganised – masculine – exciting – adventurous – needs reassurance – inspiring

…and remember: This man is not into mind games. Don't tease him or play hard to get. If you do, he'll move on to someone who demonstrates her interest more clearly.

Blind Date – speedy essentials

Who's waiting for you?
You'll probably hear him before you see him. Follow the cheerful laughter, and you'll find your date. Shy? Self-conscious? Not this guy. He's social, and talking to strangers is completely natural to him. He approaches the world with a childlike enthusiasm and curiosity; he's really a kid at heart, and there will always be something naïve and boyish about him, no matter how old he gets. As far as style is concerned, he prefers to be comfortable – but he can impress with a sharp outfit when the situation calls for it. There's no room for snobbery in his laid-back world.

Emergency fixes for embarrassing pauses
The Aries man will start the conversation. If you show him you're interested by feeding him comments and questions, he'll keep it going, and time will fly by. Mr Aries enjoys smart and intelligent women, so don't be afraid to introduce some of your own views and ideas. But don't overreach in an attempt to impress him. This guy can spot a fake quickly. You're either genuine, or you're out. Don't worry if he brings up at topic you know nothing about. Admit any gaps in knowledge, but show interest and ask some questions. He'll appreciate that.

Your place or mine?
Anyplace, really... This is an impulsive guy. Add a dose of adventure and passion, and you'll have a firework on your hands. If the chemistry is right – which is very important – then he won't need much encouragement. He doesn't like wasting his time, so don't give the impression that you're hot if you're not.

Checklist, before you dash out to meet him:
Have some fun ideas of what to eat, drink or do
(hint: be creative)
Wear a nice, casual outfit
(hint: be prepared for different venues)
Show him a photo of you in a fun place or doing something active
(hint: be interesting)
Invite him to a new boutique gym, or something similar
(hint: introduce him to something different)
Have an open mind and be positive
(hint: play along and inspire him)

Tip: This masculine, positive and enthusiastic guy can get surprisingly jealous. Be sparkling, feminine and fun, but avoid flirting with the waiter or bartender – or any guy at all.

CHAPTER 1

PREPARE YOURSELF

Catch his eye, capture his attention
Top 10 attention grabbers

1. Be cheerful and sparkling.
2. Pay attention to your looks. Emphasise your feminine – and sassy – sides.
3. Signal your interest, but don't be obvious.
4. Don't be afraid to show him your independent side.
5. Take the initiative, but without coming on too strong. He is good at picking up hints.
6. Be playful and adventurous – the one in the crowd who's up for trying out that new drink, meal, activity, etc.
7. Be confident.
8. Be hot, but be cool about it.
9. Admire and respect his masculinity, but give a little resistance.
10. Show interest in his experiences and topics of conversation.

The SHE. The woman!

An Aries man can be pretty flexible when it comes to picking a playmate for the night. On the other hand, choosing a romantic partner requires thorough attention. He expects her to be just as impulsive and enthusiastic as he is. He prefers a sporty and active woman, but she won't get far with him unless she's also classy, sassy and feminine. She must be someone he can be proud of, both in terms of looks and personality. He will lose interest if she doesn't live up to his expectations. Although he enjoys independent women, she must never challenge his masculinity.

The Essence of her
Sporty – active – feminine – has a good sense of humour - confident – charming – independent – loyal – attentive – sassy – entertaining – outgoing – can manage the fine art of charming other men without flirting – curious– loves experiencing new things – enthusiastic – impulsive – open-minded – both seeks and takes regular advice – flexible – not fussy about details – smart – has a twinkle in her eyes – positive – engaging

Aries arousal meter
From 0 to 100... In ten minutes or less. This is a passionate and erotic guy, and he's pretty flexible about where and when. Why waste time when the mood is right…?

Remember: Be true to yourself
It doesn't matter if he is the most stunning guy you've ever met – if you don't match, you don't match. You may be able to put on a show for a while to hold his attention, but what's the point? We can't please everybody. We all have different needs, dreams, tastes and preferences. There's no such thing as a one-size-fits-all lover. Be yourself, and be true to who you are – always!

Very important: Pay attention to what you say. If you manage to make him think and inspire him, you will ignite a spark in his eyes. Focus on unusual topics. Surf the net before you meet him, and gather stories with an edge.

CHAPTER 2

THE FIRST DATE

Getting your foot in the door
The basics

Whatever you are, be real. The Aries man doesn't fall for the innocent-little-girl vibe. There's a difference between being a little shy and pretending to be coy – and it's the pretending he doesn't like.

Ease into it. It's easy to relax in his company. He will take the initiative, and then it's up to you to tag along. It's like adding wood to a fire – you just have to stoke it to make sure it keeps burning.

Inspire. Introducing him to something new is a good way to pique his interest. Show him your fun, feminine and independent sides. Let him know you're not afraid to stand on your own two feet.

Cherish the masculinity. Tell him about your ideas and ask for his opinion. This is a subtle way to appeal to his masculinity.

Keep it smart and simple. If you spark his creativity and impulsiveness, the two of you may end up in all sorts of unusual places, so dress accordingly.

Whatever you do...

- **DON'T** flirt with other men when he's around.

- **DON'T** criticise his energy.

- **DON'T** bluff, overreach for compliments or tell him white lies.

- **DON'T** be loud or vulgar.

- **DON'T** put on a show or pretend to be someone you're not.

Remember, If you respond to his invitations with vague answers about needing to check you're diary, he'll be gone before you know it.

- **DON'T** play hard to get and leave him wondering what's going on.

- **DON'T** be too secretive about yourself.

- **DON'T** tease him in bed.

- **DON'T** be bossy or question his masculinity.

- **DON'T** drape yourself in a negative attitude.

The initial stages are important, but don't think too much. If it's not working out, Mr Aries will probably be the first to dash off.

Signs you're in - or not

If you're in, you'll know. If you've managed to capture his interest, he won't waste time. Getting to know you will be his first priority. He will call or text you – or both. He won't be making suggestions for next week. Prepare yourself for a 'later today' or 'tomorrow around lunch'. You'll continue scoring points with this guy if you can keep up with him and show the same level of enthusiasm. For him, life is an adventure – and it's for living. It can be quite refreshing when a guy says: I really like you. I want to see you now!

If you're not sure, or you think you may have misinterpreted something, a few signals will indicate that you've made a strong impression:

Chances are he will...

- call or text you soon after you've said goodbye
- ask for your opinion
- put projects aside to be with you
- include you in his ideas
- be protective of you and bark at men who give you the eye
- be very focused on you and unusually romantic

Not your type? Making an exit

If the two of you don't hit it off right away, he'll probably notice before you do. His social antennas are strong – especially when it comes to women. While keeping the conversation going and entertaining you with stories, he's simultaneously reading your body language and picking up on subtle cues. If you're not into him, he'll know. He moves on quickly and can even be a little blunt about it. Life is to be lived, not wasted. If you can't provide him with the excitement and adventures he's looking for, he'll hit the road.

However, if you have dazzled him with your charm, beauty and knowledge, he may continue trying to win you over. This is when you'll need to put your foot down. Sure, you could just leave, but things will go more smoothly if you help him decide for himself.

Foolproof exit measures:

These suggestions may seem a little drastic, and they may show you in a bad light – but if you really need an exit, these will get you there:

- Start talking about a new savings account you've set up that allows for no flexibility or extra spending. From now on, every little thing needs to be planned
- Tell him you find no-sex relationship fascinating
- Start giving him 'helpful' hints about everything: how to hold his glass or cutlery, the colours he's wearing, etc.
- Talk about your day in detail, including boring titbits about people he doesn't know
- Give the impression that you know very little about anything, and yawn when he tries to enlighten you
- Get giggly and silly at dinner, even if you've only had a soda

CHAPTER 3

SEX'N STUFF

Seductive moves:
How to get him in the mood:

The Aries man is usually attracted to humorous, intelligent and attractive women. However, when it comes to sex, his needs are simpler: he's turned on immediately by women who simply stare at him and say YES. He's a master of body language and knows instinctively when a woman is up for a sexual encounter. In other words, you can't really fake anything with this guy – and that means anything! However, a distracted Aries may need a little encouragement at times.

Preferences and erotic nature

An erotic suggestion out of the blue will capture an Aries man's attention. How you're dressed matters less than how you act. Hold back a little, but only for the sake of excitement. As soon as you notice a spark in his eyes, start playing and carefully teasing him. Give him room to respond. Appeal to his masculine personality by allowing him to take the lead. Just remember that the teasing stage won't last long. As soon as you've got him going, he'll be ready to release his passion.

Hitting the right buttons

Although every sign has areas that are more sensitive than others, individual sensitivity may vary quite a bit. Don't go body-blind. Honing in on these erogenous zones and forgetting the rest of him is not a good idea. Use his erogenous zones to create sparks while turning him on, and as a passion booster when it gets heated. Watch his body language – including the most obvious of signs! Open your mind to the sensuality of touch and taste.

Key areas
Face and head

Get it on
Get creative. A slight touch to his head can give him goosebumps all over. There are many opportunities to turn him on. You can do it anytime, anywhere – both at home and in public. What other people may interpret as an innocent sign of affection could actually be a seductive moment.

Arouse him
Touch him gently with the tips of your fingers, brush your lips over his ears, kiss his chin and neck, run your hands through his hair or over his head... Doing any of these softly and slowly will arouse him.

Surprise him

An erotic comment when he least expects it can spark his imagination. Follow it up with another comment a little later, and watch his smile grow. Just make sure you're prepared to follow through if you end up in a place where you can do something about it...

Spice it up

A slight variation on a traditional theme can get you far. Change the setup by getting piles of pillows that you can move around. This will enable you to experience positions from new angles.

Remember: Don't confuse his natural masculinity with dominance. He feels no need to dominate his partner – but he does take great pride in himself as a man and his ability to please his woman.

His expectations

Bring it on! He loves excitement and impulsiveness. Actually, he loves most everything – provided it's not boring.

Make it exciting. Neither time nor place matters to this guy when it comes to sex. He's not an exhibitionist, but a touch of excitement – a change of location, for example – is a sure way to spice things up. He's a perfect partner if you feel the need to shake up your erotic routine.

Keep up the pace. The Aries man approaches sex like he approaches everything in life – with energy, passion and enthusiasm. If you're looking for someone to guide you gently during sex, you'd better look elsewhere.

Be fun, be creative. His erotic mind is flexible, and he is open to suggestions. There's just one catch: he expects the same from you. He may feel disappointed if you don't go along with his ideas. If you ever find yourself in this situation, give him a few suggestions, instead – something you're into.

…and be vocal. Make sure to express your pleasure – this is very important to him.

Release your passion. In short, this is a passionate dream of a man looking for a passionate dream of a woman.

Your sensual preferences
Quiz yourself and find out whether this man is for you.

Where on the scale are you?
1 = Don't agree | 3 = Sure | 5 = Agree!

1. There's no such thing a sexual fulfillment without passion and playfulness.
One a scale for 1 to 5, you are: 1 - 2 - 3- 4 - 5

2. Being open-minded is important for expanding your erotic horizon.
One a scale for 1 to 5, you are: 1 - 2 - 3- 4 - 5

3. Too much foreplay can make sex slow and boring.
One a scale for 1 to 5, you are: 1 - 2 - 3- 4 - 5

4. Expressiveness and communication is important during sex.
One a scale for 1 to 5, you are: 1 - 2 - 3- 4 - 5

Score 15–20: Passionate, adventurous and satisfying. You're on the same level, and it's full steam ahead. Enjoy!
14–10: He may seem a bit too surprising at first, but soon, you'll enjoy exploring his erotic world and broadening your horizons.
9–5: He doesn't mind adjusting his lovemaking – provided his partner plays along.
4 – 1: While you prefer closeness, sensuality and intimacy, he charges ahead on a wave of passion. It could be fun – or it could just be a challenge.

CHAPTER 4

GENERAL STUFF

The big picture

Keep in mind that the characteristics of a Aries may vary quite a bit depending on where within the sign he was born, as well as a wide range of additional astrological factors. But for now, let's stick to the basics. Just remember: don't jump to conclusions as soon as you meet him. Give him room to shine. Get to know the man behind the sign.

His personality: Pros and cons

Pros
- Makes things happen
- Enthusiastic
- Has a good sense of humour
- Impulsive
- Confident
- Clever
- Adventurous
- Generous and kind
- Passionate
- Masculine
- Courageous
- Inspiring
- Positive and forthcoming
- Boyish and playful

Cons
- Restless
- Jealous
- Absent-minded
- Temperamental
- Childish
- Impatient
- Superficial
- Hyperactive
- Arrogant
- Indifferent
- Stubborn
- Insensitive and thoughtless
- Overly ambitious
- Enters fleeting relationships

Tip: How to show romantic interest

Suggest doing things together, and be enthusiastic, positive, assertive – and fun. Avoid being too obvious about your feelings, especially if he hasn't made up his mind about his.

Romantic Vibes

Mr Aries:
The impulsive and adventurous partner

The essence

Determined pursuit. He's just as impulsive in his romantic life as he is in every other aspect. As soon as a woman has captured his interest, the energetic Aries will make a move.

Doesn't waste time. He doesn't waste any time hanging around, contemplating. If he feels he's met the woman, he'll have no second thoughts about entering a relationship. He won't risk missing his chance.

...and sometimes a little hasty. His impulsiveness comes with a slight drawback: he doesn't always take the time to think things through. He could save himself hassle and heartbreak if he didn't always rush into the arms of love.

Opens up. A beautiful, charming and intelligent woman is like a truth serum to him: he simply needs to open up. He'll take her hand and let his emotions flow.

Spontaneous. His affection is real, but will it last? When he jumps into a relationship, he tends to forget the practical details ... like whether she's a good match for him. However, as long as his woman manages to keep up with him, admire him and inspire him, he will prove to be a warm, passionate and loyal partner.

Tip: How to show erotic interest

He can read your body language without even thinking about it, so give him a seductive smile. Think about something sensual as you look at him. Your erotic interest will shine through your eyes.

Erotic Vibrations

Mr Aries:
The passionate and playful lover

The essence

100% passion. Passion is part of who an Aries is. It flows through every cell in his body and gives him energy and enthusiasm. This applies to his erotic life as well.

Determined. He may come on a little strong and give the impression that he wants to have things his way. Don't be discouraged – this is just the passionate streak in him.

Erotically playful. He's aggressive, energetic and restless – and far from a once-a-week-under-the-covers type of guy. He is impatient and may start undressing you before you're inside the house, but he'll never be crude about it. He's simply playful and driven.

Yes! - or - No! When he initiates sex, he wants a straight yes or no. No maybes! Girls who 'need to think about it a little' won't stand a chance with him.

Express yourself. In order to feel completely satisfied, he'll need constant reassurance from you. He wants to know that you're enjoying everything as much as he is.

A new twist. He may not be a master of foreplay, but he's a creative wizard who can turn traditional positions into something new and exciting.

CHAPTER 5

COMPATIBILITY QUIZ

Are you banging your head against the wall, or does he unleash your positive potential? Do you provoke him or bring out the best in him? Does he make you throw your arms up in exasperation, or do you feel inspired and complete in his company? Are the two of you headed towards doom or dream? Take the test to find out.

Question 1.
What are the characteristics of your perfect partner?

A. Sensitive, romantic and kind.
B. Ambitious, enthusiastic and social.
C. Intense, sensual and mysterious.

Question 2.
How about you? Which of the following words best describe you?

A. Strong, creative and adventurous.
B. Down to earth, loyal and funny.
C. Dreamy, reflective and introverted.

(cont.)

Question 3.
Do you find it difficult to show your feelings?

A. No, not at all. I can talk easily about my emotions.
B. It's not that I find it difficult. I just don't see the point in rattling on about feelings all the time.
C. Sometimes, if I'm worried about not being taken seriously.

Question 4.
What would you do to show affection for your partner?

A. I'd make him a great dinner and treat him to a sensual bath later in the evening.
B. I'd take a day off and do things he finds interesting – even though I might find them a bit boring.
C. I'd buy him an expensive shirt.

Question 5.
Do you prefer to hang out with your old friends, or do you enjoy meeting new people?

A. I like hanging out with people I know well.
B. I love meeting new people – especially people who have different experiences than I do.
C. I don't mind meeting new people, but it's not especially important to me.

Question 6.
How do you feel about living for the moment and having a relaxed attitude towards budgets and finances?

A. That's not my style at all. I need financial security.
B. If you want to live in the moment, you have to spend in the moment!
C. It doesn't have to be either-or. You can be impulsive while still being financially responsible.

Question 7.
Do you enjoy a partner who is passionate and assertive in bed?

A. Yes. Sensitive little kittens are not my style.
B. Not really – too much assertiveness can ruin the emotion and reduce sex to physical workout.
C. Sure, but not every night. Closeness and tenderness are just as important.

Question 8.
Would you ever withhold sex from your partner if you were upset with him?

A. I don't like playing games. If he upset me, I'd tell him straightforwardly.
B. Yes. That's a sure way to get the message through.
C. Never. Sex is something beautiful between two people – not something you trade and bargain with.

Question 9.
What's your approach to showing interest for a guy?

A. I'd shower him with compliments, even if I don't mean half of them.
B. I'd be lively and sparkling while letting him know that I'm up-to-date on what's going on in the world.
C. I'd make it clear that I appreciate strong and adventurous men.

Question 10.
Would you describe yourself as impulsive?

A. Hmm ... not really. Planning is more my thing.
B. I can be impulsive, provided I don't need to make big decisions.
C. Absolutely. Impulsiveness can turn a grey day into an adventure.

SCORE	A	B	C
Question 1	1	10	5
Question 2	10	5	1
Question 3	10	5	1
Question 4	5	10	1
Question 5	1	10	5
Question 6	1	5	10
Question 7	10	1	5
Question 8	5	1	10
Question 9	1	10	5
Question 10	1	5	10

75 – 100
Talk about getting it right. With Mr Aries by your side, all 'life's pieces seem to fall into place. There will be excitement, positive energy, fun challenges, love and passionate sex. What else could you possibly want? You know exactly how to treat your partner to bring out the best in him – and he will reward you with all sorts of pleasures. Maybe most importantly of all, you help him organise his life so he doesn't have to worry about the details that pile up and get in his way.

51 – 74
One thing is certain: you'll never be bored with this guy. Sure, there may be discussions and even some fierce arguments, but that's just the price you pay for passion. The occasional thunderstorm will pass quickly, and you'll probably enjoy good make-up sex. You both enjoy the fact that you can speak freely with each other and never hide your feelings. You can talk to him about anything, even erotic fantasies, without feeling restricted or shy, and he appreciates your frankness. The openness in your relationship allows you to build trust and clear the air when necessary. Although he may come across as a dream, don't let him take over your life completely. He appreciates a woman who can put her foot down and give him a little resistance. Yes, he can be a little demanding at times, but for the right woman, he's a catch.

26 – 50

You're not quite sure what to make of him sometimes. Is he just a big kid with loads of charm and energy – or a childish man who needs to grow up? Don't expect him to mature overnight. The evolution of Mr Aries is a lifelong process. Some women find it fascinating and exciting; others get stressed and frustrated. If you really like him, give him a chance. Ignore the impulses that make him do things out of the blue. If you feel he's about to lose touch with reality, bring him gently down to earth. Don't fuss. You'll achieve more by being supportive and enthusiastic. But when you get tired of being a cheerleader, let him know. Tell him what you would like to do. This can actually produce positive results. This guy would prefer his woman to speak his mind, not just grumble in the background. Besides, he wants you to enjoy life as much as he does.

10 – 25

Think about it for a moment: is it possible you've confused excitement with compatibility? Did you fall for his charm without considering his true nature? It's easy to be swept away by his enthusiasm, but it could be too much to handle in the long run. Forget trying to change this man. He will always run his own show. You'll either have to adjust to his lifestyle and temperament or find someone else. A relationship that is built on a fantasy will never yield happiness. It might be a good idea to do a bit of soul searching before you make any commitments.

Thoughts...
Don't let differences discourage you. Differences may be the glue that holds a relationship together - provided you inspire each other. View the challenges from a constructive perspective.

TAURUS the male

YOUR DATE: TAURUS
21 April–20 May

The Essence of him

Handsome – masculine – charming – generous – affectionate – intelligent – stubborn – persistent – caring – loyal – classy – determined – stylish – a perfect gentleman when courting – has a strong sex-drive – traditional and a little conservative – intense – believe in the one big love – quality-conscious – goal-oriented – strong-willed – confident

...and remember: This guy can spot a fake immediately – both things and people. No matter what you do, be yourself and be genuine!

Blind Date – speedy essentials

Who's waiting for you?
There's no doubt about it: he's the stylish man with an aura of laid-back confidence who's sitting at the bar, idly swirling his drink around in his glass. He won't be obvious about it, but he'll regard you carefully before he decides to ask you to get a quick drink or treat you to dinner. He knows how to seduce women, but he can't be bothered by someone who's not up to his standards. Don't worry, he's far from arrogant – he just wants to be sure about you. This will save him – and you – from a broken heart later on.

Emergency fixes for embarrassing pauses
Be aware of any awkward moments of silence: they could be a sign that Mr Taurus is bored. He enjoys women who challenge him, provided it's not too much. Interesting questions, humorous comments and unusual points of view will sharpen his interest in you – but make sure you don't come across as a know-it-all.

Your place or mine?
This is no innocent little boy. His sex drive is strong. Although he's not seeking out casual relationships, he doesn't mind if a date night moves in a sensual direction. When and where? Doesn't really matter, as long as he feels comfortable and doesn't have to commit to breakfast.

Checklist, before you dash out to meet him:
Wear a classy detail (a watch, handbag, etc.)
(hint: no fakes)
Be up-to-date on the news
(hint: no celebrity gossip)
Look stylish and natural
(hint: no heavy perfume)
Arrive in the mood for something good to eat
(hint: no diets)
Be interesting and voice your opinions
(hint: but no fierce discussions)

Tip: Never rush this guy. Allow him to make up his mind – at his own pace. Push him, and he'll show you his stubborn side.

CHAPTER 1

PREPARE YOURSELF

Catch his eye, capture his attention
Top 10 attention grabbers

1. Admire his masculinity.
2. Wear something classy and sensual – and not too revealing.
3. Good body language and a relaxed posture.
4. Sparkling laugh and a positive personality.
5. A sensible and down-to-earth attitude.
6. Honesty is a must! Any evasiveness will leave him frustrated and impatient.
7. Make sure to have an open mind and don't be fixed in your views.
8. Let him know you've made an effort before seeing him – look good.
9. Intelligent comments and questions will cause him to pay attention.
10. Compliments work well, but only if they are sincere. He will quickly call your bluff.

The SHE. The woman!

Although a Taurus man may fall for a pretty face and a sleek body, inner beauty is just as important to him – probably even more so. However, this doesn't mean that his ideal woman will ever let herself go. Looks are important to him – but they're not the only thing. Superficial women have no room in his life. His partner must be a little bit of everything: soft, feminine, independent, strong, loyal and intelligent, with a well-developed sense of humour. He needs someone he can trust and rely on, not a social butterfly or a bar-babe.

The Essence of her

Smart – compassionate – fit, with a healthy outlook on life – intelligent – independent – loyal and supportive – sensual – strong – feminine – has a good sense of humour – grounded – classy – appreciative of family life – assertive in her professional life – appreciates the finer things – a good hostess – charming in social settings – a reliable team player – passionate and romantic

Taurus arousal meter

From 0 to 100... In five seconds – or two hours! There are no rules. This man is either-or. But with the right encouragement, his erotic intensity may sparkle like a firework.

Remember: Be true to yourself
It doesn't matter if he is the most stunning guy you've ever met – if you don't match, you don't match. You may be able to put on a show for a while to hold his attention, but what's the point? We can't please everybody. We all have different needs, dreams, tastes and preferences. There's no such thing as a one-size-fits-all lover. Be yourself, and be true to who you are – always!

Very important: Never tease him or play hard to get. If you hint at one thing but do the opposite, you'll just end up confusing him – and losing him.

CHAPTER 2

THE FIRST DATE

Getting your foot in the door
The basics

No aggressiveness, please. Don't throw yourself at him. Guide him gently with hints and suggestive glances, but don't be too obvious about your interest. If he finds you interesting, he will connect the dots very quickly.

The beauty within. He appreciates style and physical looks, but inner beauty is just as important.

Keep it discreet. A small touch of luxury can be attractive, but don't overdo it. You don't want to come across as someone who throws money around.

Never fake it. Don't wear fake designer goods and pretend they are real. He has no room for fakes in his life – whether things or people.

No negative stuff. Keep the conversation bright, positive and optimistic. Talking about depressing stuff in the news will give him a headache.

Intelligent flattery. If you can draw positive attention to something about him that isn't obvious, you will score points.

Whatever you do...

- **DON'T** become overly engaged during discussions.

- **DON'T** make promises you can't keep. He won't forget.

- **DON'T** wear too much perfume or makeup. Keep it natural.

- **DON'T** try to impress him with fake bling.

- **DON'T** take his generosity for granted.

Remember,
Take the initiative and show interest. If he pampers you without getting anything in

- **DON'T** rush him – about anything.

- **DON'T** lie – not even little white lies.

- **DON'T** be secretive. Evasiveness annoys him endlessly.

- **DON'T** be picky about food or fuss about being on a diet.

- **DON'T** express your feelings with subtle hints. He'll either get it wrong or not notice at all.

return, he's liable to lose interest and disappear.

Signs you're in - or not

The Taurus man is an either-or kind of guy: he's either interested or he's not. The specific kind of interest, however, depends on your first date. If you had a hot and erotic date, it could be that he's simply looking for more of the same. If sex hasn't entered the picture but the two of you got on really well, there are foolproof signals that you have sparked his interest. There's no need to interpret anything. There are no hidden messages. This guy is blunt and straightforward. Look out for the following:

Chances are he will...

- call you as soon as he gets a chance
- suggest seeing you again as soon as possible
- pay you compliments and show an interest in what you're doing
- give you a little something to show that he cares
- act playfully jealous of other men (he might actually be a little jealous)
- make an effort to impress you: a homemade meal, a special drink, a reservation somewhere nice...

Not your type? Making an exit

Leaving a Taurus man can be a challenge – it depends how hooked he is. Although he may have a casual attitude toward sex, he seldom drifts from one romantic relationship to another. If he has decided to spend time and energy on you, he's doing it for a reason –he likes you. When a man born under the sign of Taurus makes up his mind, he is prepared to apply his patience and persistence to making things work – even if you think it's pointless…

However, there are limits to how far Mr Taurus is willing to go – how much rubbish he is willing to tolerate, and how much stupidity he can live with every day. Take it upon yourself to look bad, and the exit ought to be smooth and quick.

Foolproof exit measures:

Think twice before trying out any of the suggestions below. Besides making you look bad, some are downright mean.

- No more sex! Blame whatever. Headaches. Work. The colour of his socks.
- Criticise his sex drive and tell him to cool down.
- Turn everything into a discussion: big issues, tiny details, anything.
- Insist that he go on a diet.
- Spend money on fake designer items, and claim you thought they were real.
- Tell him to hurry up, no matter what he's doing

CHAPTER 3

SEX'N STUFF

Seductive moves:
How to get him in the mood:

Never be impatient with this guy. You can nudge him carefully, but never, ever push him. Luckily, when it comes to sex, you probably won't have to. If he doesn't respond to your erotic invitation, he's probably knocked out with the flu.

Preferences and erotic nature

Sex is important to a Taurus man on many levels. It's a source of energy, inspiration and relaxation – as well as a potent confirmation of his masculinity (not that he needs any confirmation … you're dealing with is a confident guy). This masculine approach leaves a lot up to him, and he enjoys taking the initiative and being in charge. However, he feeds on feedback from his partner! This is important. For him, there is no such thing as sex without pleasing his partner, and he wants to be sure he's doing just that. A seemingly indifferent woman – even just a quiet woman – can turn him off completely.

Hitting the right buttons

Although every sign has areas that are more sensitive than others, individual sensitivity may vary quite a bit. Don't go body-blind. Honing in on these erogenous zones and forgetting the rest of him is not a good idea. Use his erogenous zones to create sparks while turning him on, and as a passion booster when it gets heated. Watch his body language – including the most obvious of signs! Open your mind to the sensuality of touch and taste.

Key areas
His throat and neck

Get it on
You can spark his interest anytime, anywhere, without making it obvious to the people around you! The sensitivity of his throat and the neck provide endless opportunities to 'accidentally' heat him up. If you're out in public, be casual about it. Make him wonder about your intentions.

Arouse him
Carefully touch him while adjusting his sweater, tie or jacket. Allow the tips of your fingers to gently brush against the back of his neck while sitting next to him on a bus or in a taxi. And obviously: soft lips or the tip of your tongue gently playing along his throat during sex will act as a nice passion-booster.

Surprise him

When it comes to sex, he's pretty much ready anytime, and on short notice. But with a little creativity, it's still possible to surprise him. Suggest an erotic encounter in an unusual place when he least expects it. Big bonus if you're by yourselves, surrounded by nature…

Spice it up

He is a very sensual being, and you can play to this. Try adding an element of taste during foreplay, like whipped cream or chocolate. For smell, pleasant – and lightly scented! – aromatic oils are perfect for a sensual massage.

Remember: He doesn't really need reassurance, but he appreciates a partner who recognizes him as a wonderful and passionate lover. Be vocal.

His expectations

Be ready. He expects a woman to be sensually spontaneous and play along when the erotic temperature is on the rise.

Embrace his passion. A woman who doesn't enjoy an erotic man, should go looking for someone else. The Taurus male needs a woman who appreciates his passion. Too many rejections will turn him off his partner.

No hard core! Although he does have a liberal streak, he does not appreciate anything vulgar in bed.

Femininity rules! His partner needs to be tender, sensual and passionate. Wearing feminine and slightly sassy underwear is a nice touch.

Participate. A passive partner is a major turn off. She must actively participate and let him know clearly that she appreciates what he's doing.

Sensuality. He uses his senses actively during sex, and he enjoys the natural scents of a woman – not a body showered with perfume. Strong artificial smells can ruin the overall experience for him.

Your sensual preferences
Quiz yourself and find out whether this man is for you.

Where on the scale are you?
1 = Don't agree | 3 = Sure | 5 = Agree!

1. Expressing passion is very important during sex.
One a scale for 1 to 5, you are : 1 - 2 - 3- 4 - 5

2. Having sex in new places can add erotic dimensions.
One a scale for 1 to 5, you are : 1 - 2 - 3- 4 - 5

3. Frequent sex is important in order to thrive.
One a scale for 1 to 5, you are : 1 - 2 - 3- 4 - 5

4. Too much romantic sensitivity ruins the excitement of sex.
One a scale for 1 to 5, you are : 1 - 2 - 3- 4 - 5

Score 15–20: Hot and steamy. Spontaneous and exciting. Never, ever boring!
Score 10–14: He may be a bit much at times, but you're probably up for it!
Score 5–9: Let him know what pleases you. Guide him, but don't criticise.
Score 1–4: You may feel overwhelmed by this guy. Make sure to tell him about your preferences before jumping into bed.

CHAPTER 4

GENERAL STUFF

The big picture

Keep in mind that the characteristics of a Taurus may vary quite a bit depending on where within the sign he was born, as well as a wide range of additional astrological factors. But for now, let's stick to the basics. Just remember: don't jump to conclusions as soon as you meet him. Give him room to shine. Get to know the man behind the sign.

His personality: Pros and cons

Pros
- Loyal and supportive
- Romantic
- Kind
- Masculine
- Passionate
- Persistent and assertive
- Humorous
- Determined
- Has an eye for quality
- Confident
- Enjoys the good things in life
- Charming
- Frank
- Erotic
- Down-to-earth

Cons
- Stubborn
- Slow
- Rigid
- Lazy
- Dwells on the past
- Possessive
- Pushy
- Ignorant
- Arrogant
- A womaniser
- Argumentative
- Patronizing
- Demanding
- Critical
- Has a low tolerance for criticism

Tip: How to show romantic interest

Taking interest in what he's doing is a good start. Making an effort to do something nice, like preparing dinner or giving him a gift that's a little out of the ordinary, will make him realise he's got something good going on...

Romantic Vibes

Mr Taurus:
The romantic and attentive partner

The essence

The knight in shining armour. He can be a real chivalrous gentleman. In his mind, he sometimes sees himself as a knight, looking for a princess to rescue. In the real world, he's still a man – but he's quite a catch, and he knows it.

Choosy. Don't think you've captured this guy just because you've had one hot date. Sex and love are two different things for this man, and he's choosier about who he lets into his heart than who he lets into his bedroom.

Pamper his woman. If you have managed to capture his romantic attention, you have a lot to look forward to. He will treat you like a princess, spoiling you with little gifts and loads of tender attention.

Showing you off. The moment he's your guy, he won't hesitate to show you off to the world. He will be proud of you.

Intimacy is important. He is a romantic with a fondness for the intimacy he can create when he's alone with his partner. And he's is open to suggestions!

Knows his stuff. Mr Taurus is kind, loyal, intense, passionate – and stubborn. He's also an extremely charming man who knows how to take care of his woman.

Tip: How to show erotic interest

That's easy. A glance, a smile, a sweet comment... His erotic antennas are finely tuned, and he will pick up on erotic interest right away. He doesn't get coy flirtation. Either you want to have sex, or you don't.

Erotic Vibrations

Mr Taurus:
The passionate and determined lover

The essence

When he's hot, he's hot! Don't expect him to be a sweet and sensitive lover who holds back his own desires to wait for the right moment. As soon as you have sparked his passion, he's ready to go…

If you start something, finish it. If you don't want to have sex, don't tease him. If you do, you can wave goodbye to future dates.

Be genuine. Mr Taurus expects people to be genuine on all fronts. Saying one thing and doing something different does not go down well with him – in any area of life!

Strong sex drive. He's usually patient, but not when it comes to sex. His sex drive is strong. If he could work out in bed rather that at the gym, he'd probably do it.

Don't make it complicated. More sensitive guys may be inclined to use sex to communicate feelings and tenderness with their partners. Not this guy. He appreciates sex for its own sake.

His partner is queen! He doesn't get pleasure from sex unless his partner enjoys it as much as he does. His number one is to make sure she is happy.

CHAPTER 5

COMPATIBILITY QUIZ

Are you banging your head against the wall, or does he unleash your positive potential? Do you provoke him or bring out the best in him? Does he make you throw your arms up in exasperation, or do you feel inspired and complete in his company? Are the two of you headed towards doom or dream? Take the test to find out.

Question 1.
How would you feel about a guy who made erotic advances when you least expected it?

A. Not really my thing. I don't like sexually intense guys.
B. That would depend on my mood. I guess it could be fun…
C. I'd love it! I love spontaneity, excitement and never knowing when it's going to happen.

Question 2.
Do you enjoy good food?

A. Food itself is no big deal. A nice atmosphere and good company are far more important.
B. Food is fuel. I don't understand why people make such a fuss about it.
C. I love cooking – bringing out new flavours, trying new things.

(cont.)

Question 3.
As a lover, which of these keywords fits you the best?

A. Playful and active.
B. Intense and passionate.
C. Passive and conservative.

Question 4.
Which of these keywords fits your ideal partner?

A. Grounded, intense, masculine.
B. Determined, creative, adventurous.
C. Dreamy, romantic, sensitive.

Question 5.
Do you think it's important to support and encourage your partner when the world turns against him?

A. Of course! Everyone needs a supportive partner.
B. Well, I try to do that … but he doesn't seem to need it.
C. No need. The man in my life is strong and capable of taking care of himself.

Question 6.
What's the first thing that springs to mind when you see the words 'whipped cream'?

A. A big dessert with loads of calories?
B. A very sensual evening…
C. Fun, games, mess and laughter

Question 7.
How do you tend to show your love for your partner?

A. I tell him how I feel.
B. I usually pamper him a little: buy him a gift or give him a massage.
C. He knows I love him. No need to rattle on about it all the time.

Question 8.
You've decided to get some work done. How do you respond when your partner lights a candle, opens a bottle of wine and gives you a suggestive look?

A. It would really annoy me, especially if he knew I had work to do.
B. I expect that he'd manage to persuade me to take a break.
C. I'd love it. This is one of the things that make my partner so special.

Question 9.
Do you think it's important to show affection in bed?

A. I prefer hot passion that leaves little room for tenderness and affection.
B. Of course. Sex without affection is cold and impersonal.
C. It depends. Sometimes things are passionate and steamy; other times it's close, sweet and affectionate.

Question 10
Do you ever take the initiative to spice things up in the bedroom?

A. Yes, often. My partner seems to appreciate the initiative.
B. Never. I don't regard myself as sexually aggressive.
C. Sometimes, but it's never anything too extreme.

SCORE	A	B	C
Question 1	1	5	10
Question 2	5	1	10
Question 3	5	10	1
Question 4	10	5	1
Question 5	10	5	1
Question 6	1	10	5
Question 7	5	10	1
Question 8	1	5	10
Question 9	1	5	10
Question 10	10	1	5

75 – 100
This is a perfect match, but you probably knew that already. You may be quite different, but both of your fundamental values are strong. It's almost as if you share a subconscious understanding, and all it takes to communicate is a look and a smile. Exploring life's pleasures is important: art, food, sex… The ability to discover joy and adventure in the smallest of things makes this relationship happy, exciting and unique.

51 – 74
From simple bliss to exciting challenges, this relationship will never be boring. You may provoke each other at times, but you never seem to cross the line. Instead of getting on each other's nerves, you inspire one another and bring energy to the relationship. Your differences may make you stronger as individuals, but they will bring you closer as a couple. Flexibility and patience are important for making this relationship flourish – but you knew that already. Take time seize the moment and embrace the pleasures. It will bring a wonderful dimension to the relationship.

26 – 50

One thing is certain: this relationship will never be boring. Some people love intense energy ... but it takes two to tango. If one of you finds it difficult to keep up with the other, the whole thing can become draining. Or it could be that you both apply your energy to different areas of your life – the same problem will arise. In order for this to work, you'll need to figure out whether you're able to channel your energy in the same direction. If you manage to find a common ground, you'll still need to be honest with each other – and true to yourselves. Love is a powerful thing, but if you feel there's more nagging than hugging going on here, it might be better to opt for a close and strong friendship.

10 – 25

It may have been fun at first. It may even have been passionate and exciting. But how do you feel now? Certain experiences in life are meant to be passing. This adventure may be one of them. Embrace the excitement of a new experience, and leave it at that. True harmony and lasting romantic love will be found elsewhere. Life is for living, and we need to surround ourselves with people who bring out the best in us. Start looking...

Suggestion
Never hold on to something just for the sake of it. Make sure there is a good reason for what you do - and that whatever you do brings you happiness.

GEMINI the male

YOUR DATE: GEMINI
21 May–20 June

The Essence of him

Convincing – enthusiastic – social – kind – fast-paced – individualistic – smart – eloquent – superficial – restless – able to multitask – impatient – easily distracted – needs people around him – seeks inspiration and input – loves traveling and exploring new turf – has a dualistic personality – dynamic – boyishly charming – attentive – open-minded

...and remember: This is a restless guy who is easily bored. He's always moving forward and needs constant inspiration in order to thrive.

Blind Date – speedy essentials

Who's waiting for you?
You probably won't notice him right away: the classily dressed That guy over there – yes, the one who's already talking to a couple of other women – either ones he has just met, or a couple of his girlfriends. However, as soon as he sees you, the other women will disappear from his mind. Now he's totally focused on you – well, as long you manage to hold his attention. This shouldn't be a problem, because this is a curious guy who is very interested in people. He's kind, but also restless, both physically and mentally. If you're not used to fast-paced mental activity, he may come across as a little hasty. But hasty or not, this is a very entertaining guy.

Emergency fixes for embarrassing pauses
Embarrassing pauses? Forget it. This man can talk about several things at the same time without losing track of any of them. He will expect you to follow along as he leaps from one subject to the other. He loves interesting news and sassy gossip. If you've got a good story up your sleeve, tell it and you'll have his full attention.

Your place or mine?
The Gemini man is not fixated on sex. However, if the situation should arise... then sure, why not? He is just as impulsive about sex as he is about everything else. But in his world, love and sex are not necessarily connected. Sex on the first date doesn't ensure a call the next day. This man is an expert when it comes to casual hook-ups.

Checklist, before you dash out to meet him:

Keep an open mind, with no fixed expectations
(hint: Don't make him feel cornered)
Prepare ideas about things to do and places to go
(hint: Keep it interesting)
Maintain a positive self-image
(hint: Don't be put off by competition)
Don't dwell on recent break-ups
(hint: Be sparkling and playful)
Know some good stories and fun facts
(hint: Be entertaining)

Tip: This is a fast-moving guy – especially mentally . You'll need to be on your toes to keep up with him. Hold his attention with interesting facts and good stories.

CHAPTER 1

PREPARE YOURSELF

Catch his eye, capture his attention
Top 10 attention grabbers

1. Take the initiative to approach him.
2. Be fun and sparkling. Looking good is not enough.
3. Be playful and show affection – without getting clingy.
4. Impress him with your knowledge.
5. Be outgoing and chat charmingly with other men.
6. Suggest going somewhere fun.
7. Don't be shy about erotic topics.
8. Spark his curiosity by talking about something exotic.
9. Don't be too obvious about your interest. Make him wonder.
10. Offer him a little gossip. He likes it, although he may not admit it.

The SHE. The woman!

The Gemini man is looking for a companion. He wants someone who can join him along the journey of life; someone who is open-minded and embraces everything life has to offer; someone who can inspire him – inside and outside the bedroom! Restless by nature, he doesn't have the patience to sit around and wait for his dream woman to arrive. He is impulsive and gets carried away by interesting women.

The Essence of her
Spontaneous – strong – independent – interesting, never boring – represents a challenge – intelligent –adaptable – fun and humorous – has a positive attitude about life – erotically liberated – enthusiastic – outgoing and social – well-informed, with her own views – entertaining – not afraid of voicing her opinions – attractive

---

Gemini arousal meter
From 0 to 100... In 10, 15, 20 minutes … if his thoughts are all over the place, he may need a while to focus.

Remember: Be true to yourself
It doesn't matter if he is the most stunning guy you've ever met – if you don't match, you don't match. You may be able to put on a show for a while to hold his attention, but what's the point? We can't please everybody. We all have different needs, dreams, tastes and preferences. There's no such thing as a one-size-fits-all lover. Be yourself, and be true to who you are – always!

Very important: Don't get too comfy in his company. He will lose interest if you start taking it for granted. Make an effort.

CHAPTER 2

THE FIRST DATE

Getting your foot in the door
The basics

Beauty *and* brains. Looks are important, but they're not everything. You may have a hard time catching this guy if you're used to relying on your appearance. He may show interest, but if you've got nothing more to offer, he'll be off.

Be stimulating. He prefers engaging women that he can have a discussion with.

Better catch him before he's gone. Don't wait for him to make the first move. This is a popular guy, and if you don't take the initiative, someone else will. Be charming, enthusiastic and entertaining.

Show an interest. As soon as you've got his attention, pick up on his interests and start talking about them.

Don't be shy, be smart. He likes smart women who impress him with knowledge about art, music and what's going on.

Dish a little gossip. He likes gossip because it brings a touch of sensation, so juicy stories are good, too – but steer clear of the negative ones.

Whatever you do...

- **DON'T** rely on a sexy outfit to get his attention.

- **DON'T** be loud and aggressive.

- **DON'T** be too conservative in your ways (manners, etc.).

- **DON'T** be argumentative and fixed in your opinions.

- **DON'T** give the impression you are erotically inhibited.

Remember, Although he may seem very interested, never take his interest for granted.

- **DON'T** refuse to taste a certain food because you may not like it.

- **DON'T** be negative or critical.

- **DON'T** interrupt him. Listen and pay attention.

- **DON'T** be clingy. Give him space.

- **DON'T** get jealous when he chats with other women.

If he gets bored, he'll cut and run.

Signs you're in - or not

It can be tricky to figure out where you stand with this man, simply because he's so charming – to everybody. He may go out with you, have a great time and even sleep with you if the mood turns hot and steamy, but none of that guarantees that he's really into you. If you don't manage to trigger his curiosity, he will move on to the next female adventure in his life. This may sound like a challenge, but it doesn't have to be. Just be smart about it. If he's keen on getting to know you further, the signs will be clear:

Chances are he will...

- approach you with charm and boyish enthusiasm
- talk positively about you to others when you're out with him
- ask for your opinion and leave decisions up to you
- make an effort to please you
- call you just to chat
- be more interested in hanging out with you than his friends

Not your type? Making an exit

Getting rid of a Gemini? No problem at all. This freedom-loving, adventure-seeking free spirit will say goodbye as soon as there's a hint of boredom in the air. He believes that life is for living, exploring and enjoying, and remaining in a stagnant relationship is against the fundaments of his nature. It would make him miserable – and he is not a man to hang around and sulk. He very much takes ownership of his own happiness and will quickly move on if things aren't working out.

Exceptions to the rule are rare. It could be that you have dazzled him so much that he has lost touch with reality. He could lack initiative, feel too comfortable or be hoping that he can change you. But if his constant need for speed is driving you nuts, it's time to get the message through.

Foolproof exit measures:

These suggestions will make him go 'What?!' You may want to add a little extra passion, just to make sure it sinks in – and it probably will…!

- Be jealous of everyone. Text him constantly to ask where he is.
- Make sure to be the centre of attention when you're out with friends.
- Criticize his ideas and tell him to be more thorough
- Insist on having sex with the lights out – and no sassy stuff, please!
- Restrict his freedom by demanding that he spend more time with you.
- Tell him to stop flirting when he's being friendly to other women.

CHAPTER 3

SEX'N STUFF

Seductive moves:
How to get him in the mood:

It would probably be easier to figure out what he doesn't like to do in bed – this guy is more or less into anything. His motto is: 'I'll try anything once, and twice if I like it!' ...and he usually does. Any suggestion that's a little out of the ordinary, or comes at a surprising time, will bring a sparkle to his eyes.

Preferences and erotic nature

The Gemini man will have sex anywhere. He's not an inhibited guy, and the chances of being seen can actually increase his excitement. He'll try all sorts of things to bring new angles to his sex life: from positions to gadgets to locations. Be straightforward with him – he will appreciate that. If there are sexual activities you don't enjoy, let him know and he will immediately come up with several different suggestions. This man is serious about pleasing; failure to do so is not an option in his world. In fact, he loves asking his partner to please herself while he watches her. However, this only works if she's ready for it. If she is shy, he will try something else.

Hitting the right buttons

Although every sign has areas on the body that are more sensitive than others, individual sensitivity may vary quite a bit. Don't go body-blind. Honing in on these erogenous zones and forgetting the rest of him is not a good idea. Use these areas to create sparks while turning him on, and as a passion-booster when things get heated. Watch his body language – including the most obvious of signs. Open your mind to the sensuality of touch and taste.

Key areas
Hands and fingers

Get it on
When you shake his hand, be aware that you are touching a part of his body that sends erotic signals to his brain. Depending on the situation, you can actually accomplish a lot through simple hand contact. But remember, this man can be ready on short notice. Don't indicate erotic interest if you don't intend to see it through.

Arouse him
Whenever you touch his hands and fingers, use warm, tender and sensual movements. How? Easy. If you want to arouse him in public, let your hands and fingers 'accidentally' brush against his. If you want to let him know that you have other things in mind than conversation, carefully scratch his hands and fingers with your fingernails – and don't forget the skin between his fingers. Gentle kisses and a brush with the tip of your tongue should make him start to breathe a little quicker...

Surprise him
If you're usually not too vocal in bed, catch him off-guard by whispering a few naughty suggestions into his ear. This will always make him hot – and no need to be particularly creative. The sheer seductiveness of your voice will do the trick.

Spice it up
Bring mirrors into the bedroom. This is a visual guy, and he will get a kick out of exploring you from different angles all at once.

Remember: Although he may come across as erotic and adventurous, he will never want to do anything his partner doesn't appreciate.

His expectations

Expect a lot of energy. He is all about activity, interest and initiative!

Never take it easy. There is no such thing as lying back and expecting a Gemini man to run the show. A passive woman will never excite him.

Keep an open mind. He appreciates someone who is open to new ideas, and who doesn't criticize him when he comes up with new and 'interesting' suggestions.

Lights on, please. He is visually driven, and having sex with the lights out removes an important aspect of his lovemaking. Don't be surprised if he suggests adding a few mirrors around the room.

Playful triggers. You don't have to be an erotic expert to please him. A playful, open and enthusiastic partner will bring out the best in him.

Aims to please. He really wants to be regarded as a good lover. He will work hard to please you – but he will expect you to do the same if you want to keep him around.

Your sensual preferences
Quiz yourself and find out whether this man is for you.

Where on the scale are you?
1 = Don't agree | 3 = Sure | 5 = Agree!

1. Sex can be enjoyed on its own merit, and not only as an expression of romantic feelings.
One a scale for 1 to 5, you are: 1 - 2 - 3- 4 - 5

2. New ideas are important for maintaining a satisfying sex life.
One a scale for 1 to 5, you are: 1 - 2 - 3- 4 - 5

3. In order to fully enjoy sex, the visual aspect is very important.
One a scale for 1 to 5, you are: 1 - 2 - 3- 4 - 5

4. Too much closeness and intimacy can ruin the excitement of sex.
One a scale for 1 to 5, you are: 1 - 2 - 3- 4 - 5

Score 15–20: This will be an ongoing erotic adventure – never boring and always satisfying.
Score 10–14: He may surprise you with unusual suggestions, but that's one of the things that makes sex with him so exciting.
Score 5–9: You may find him a bit too body-focused at times. Let him know what you like. He wants to please his partner – provided your interests are compatible.
Score 1–4: If his playful creativity doesn't knock you off your feet in pleasure, it may send you running for the door.

CHAPTER 4

GENERAL STUFF

The big picture

Keep in mind that the characteristics of a Gemini may vary quite a bit depending on where within the sign he was born, as well as a wide range of additional astrological factors. But for now, let's stick to the basics. Just remember: don't jump to conclusions as soon as you meet him. Give him room to shine. Get to know the man behind the sign.

His personality: Pros and cons

Pros
- Boyish
- Charming
- Dynamic
- Social
- Smart
- Eloquent
- Persuasive
- Enthusiastic
- Individualistic
- Kind
- Supportive
- Playful
- Positive
- Constructive

Cons
- Restless
- Superficial
- Emotionally reserved
- Indecisive
- Has superficial relationships
- Conflict-avoidant
- Afraid of romantic commitment
- Blunt
- A flirt and a player
- Impatient
- Has a low threshold for criticism
- Doesn't see things through
- Ignores negative feedback
- Drifts from one thing to another

Tip: How to show romantic interest

Be sparkling, make an effort to learn about the things he is interested in and keep him wondering how you really feel about him – at least until the time is right.

Romantic Vibes

Mr Gemini:
The enthusiastic and restless partner

The essence

Embrace love. The Gemini man seldom thinks twice about entering into a relationship if a woman has sparked his romantic interest. He expects her to be just as charming and mentally stimulating as the first time he met her. He will leave as soon as he starts getting bored.

Freedom and trust. He really dislikes jealous women. His ideal partner must never criticize him for having female friends or get angry when he flirts.

From love to logic. His feelings are governed by his mind, not his heart. If the relationship starts to close in on him, he will transform his romantic feelings into logical thoughts and find a way to make an exit.

Her pleasure, my command. He is an exciting partner who will turn the world upside down in order to please his woman.

Don't outshine him. He would be insulted if his woman got all the attention. She must shine, but allow him to take centre stage.

Tip: How to show erotic interest

Tell him about an article you've just read about positions that are supposed to increase pleasure during sex. Just let him know you thought it was quite interesting...

Erotic Vibrations

Mr Gemini:
The adventurous and playful lover

The essence

Fun and adventure. He is a restless lover with a playful twinkle in his eyes. This is a smart guy, and he knows exactly how to seduce a woman – even if she's a little shy.

No sweaty sessions. Intense passion is not really his thing. He's interested in performance and excitement, but that does not make him a cold and insensitive lover – far from it.

Adding spice. He is adventurous and always willing to try something new. Don't be surprised if you find a few gadgets and sex toys in his bedroom.

Skip the boring stuff. Traditional lovemaking tends to bore him after a while, and he may come up with new suggestions.

Indecisive... His slightly split personality applies to his sex life, as well. A part of him wants to explore sex without commitment. The other side longs for a more stable life and a long-term partner.

Erotic fun. If you have just met him and are serious about him, be careful. Although he may seem sincere about you, he may also be off first thing the next morning. However, if you just want to have some erotic fun, go for it!

CHAPTER 5

COMPATIBILITY QUIZ

Are you banging your head against the wall, or does he unleash your positive potential? Do you provoke him or bring out the best in him? Does he make you throw your arms up in exasperation, or do you feel inspired and complete in his company? Are the two of you headed towards doom or dream? Take the test to find out.

Question 1.
Do you enjoy having lots of things going on, or do you prefer to focus on one thing at the time?

A. Doing things thoroughly is very important to me – and that's impossible if you have too much going on.
B. I enjoy doing several things at once, but I admit that I'm not always that focused.
C. I need activity to thrive. I have no problem focusing on a few things simultaneously.

Question 2.
Summer is just around the corner, but your budget is limited. How will you spend your vacation?

A. I'd always try to experience and explore something new – no matter what my budget might be.
B. In the peace and quiet, camping somewhere nearby.
C. A staycation could be fun – exploring the area, the neighbourhoods and all the things I've been meaning to do for a long time.

(cont.)

Question 3.
You're having dinner at your Gemini's place. How do you respond when the doorbell rings and you hear him say: 'Tom! Peter! I haven't seen you in ages! Come in! Come in!'?

A. I like doing things at the spur of the moment, and it would be nice to meet his friends. We could always do a romantic dinner another day.
B. What? That is so insensitive. I'd put on my coat and leave.
C. Just typical ... I wouldn't be thrilled, but his spontaneity is also one of the things I find attractive about him.

Question 4.
Do you think it's important to have constant variation in your sex life?

A. I don't want my sex life to be hectic, but I don't want it to become a boring routine, either. I like a nice balance.
B. Absolutely! Having an exciting sex life provides me with renewed energy.
C. The constant quest for new sexual pleasures wears me out. I prefer calm and quiet sex.

Question 5.
In a relationship, do you get jealous?

A. No, not at all.
B. Very seldom.
C. Yes. I'd never tolerate my boyfriend spending time with female friends.

Question 6.
What do you usually do when you run into a problem?

A. Start worrying.
B. Face the issue head-on and find a solution.
C. Call a friend and ask for advice and assistance.

Question 7.
Do you tend to get carried away by enthusiastic ideas?

A. No. I'm very focused, and I keep my feet on the ground.
B. Sometimes, but only if the topic really captures my interest.
C. Absolutely! Any new idea could be a major success just waiting to happen.

Question 8.
Do you find it boring to take turns pleasing each other during sex?

A. Depends on my mood, really. Sometimes I prefer straight-to-the-point sex.
B. Not at all. By taking turns, you really get to enjoy each other.
C. Yes. I'm more into the sensual side of sex, where things are more mutual.

Question 9.
Do you tend to be shy in bed?

A. Not at all. I actually prefer to make love with the lights on.
B. Maybe a little, if the relationship is still new.
C. Yes. I'm a little body-conscious.

Question 10.
Do you find it easy to talk about sex?

A. Why would you want to talk about sex? Sex should be explored and enjoyed physically, not verbally.
B. Yes, provided that the setting is right. There's a time and place for everything.
C. Yes. I love talking about sex. It inspires me.

SCORE	A	B	C
Question 1	1	5	10
Question 2	10	1	5
Question 3	10	1	5
Question 4	5	10	1
Question 5	10	5	1
Question 6	1	10	5
Question 7	1	5	10
Question 8	5	10	1
Question 9	10	5	1
Question 10	1	5	10

75 – 100

Bliss – but not in the traditional, lackadaisical sense of the word. You don't spend the days gazing into each other's eyes. You're out there, living, exploring, enjoying and creating a bond between two individualists. He makes you shine. You inspire him and bring out his potential . The communication between you is unique: with a quick glance across a room full of people, you know exactly what he's thinking. If he's not you dream man, he comes pretty close. Enjoy!

51 – 74

Although he does wear you out from time to time, he still creates an aura of happiness around you. He brings your days to life and fills them with excitement. Neither of you wants a relationship that requires you to spend every minute in each other's company – but you seem to spend a lot of time together anyway. This is partiall because you share the same values and expectations – as well as the joy of exploring new horizons. Boredom will never be an issue for you two. Although you may stumble from time to time, you will learn from each other and continue to grow. Embrace the journey.

26 – 50

How much are you prepared to sacrifice? Are you strong enough to keep your cool when Mr Gemini takes off and doesn't call you for a week? Are you sure this is the man you want in your life, or are you confusing love with excitement? Sure, he's charming, good-looking and fun. He brings energy to your life and makes you feel alive. But does he really satisfy you? Are your most important needs being fulfilled? Love can conquer all, but are you sure this is worth it? It's important to find the right balance. If you feel like one of you is surfing through life while the other is waiting on the beach, something is definitely missing. Be true to yourself and go looking for a man who puts your needs first.

10 – 25

How could two so completely different people end up in each other's company? This is surely one of life's greatest mysteries. Maybe it's a classic case of 'opposites attract', or maybe he touched something within you that made you experience life differently? But the same qualities that struck you as exciting a while ago may now seem like a hassle – for both of you. Perhaps you find him restless and superficial, and he wants you to be more flexible and impulsive. You're pulling in opposite directions and holding each other back. It's time to explore happiness elsewhere.

Thoughts...
Sometimes we have to make an effort, open up and give a little.

Challenges could be opportunities for the relationship to improve and get stronger.

CANCER the male

YOUR DATE: CANCER
21 June–22 July

The Essence of him

Masculine – elegant – stylish – reserved – polite – attentive – patient – sympathetic – caring – compassionate – sensitive – moody – has strong bonds with friends and family – sensible – goal-oriented – ambitious – has a good memory – intensely feeling – insecure – kind – considerate – empathetic – jealous – big-hearted – romantic – a dreamer – a good listener

...and remember: Although he is strong and masculine, it's important for the Cancer male to receive reassurance. Never leave him wondering about your feelings or your intentions. That'll make him insecure and miserable.

Blind Date – speedy essentials

Who's waiting for you?
Stylish and relaxed, with a broad smile ... there's no doubt about it, this is a manly man. His masculinity shines through his personality, not through a tight-fitting t-shirt. He is naturally gallant, polite and attentive: it's as though he was born to be a gentleman. You'll find no macho tendencies, no raucous laughter or silly jokes, no intense and analysing stares. He will do his best to make you feel relaxed and at ease in his company. However, don't expect too much from his outfit. This is no fashion icon. He prefers to keep it casual.

Emergency fixes for embarrassing pauses
Don't worry about pauses. As soon as he has eased into the role, he will gladly guide you through conversation and ask questions to help you loosen up a bit. Pauses will usually only occur if the two of you don't have anything in common. Be positive and entertaining. He will notice the vibes, and everything will flow freely and naturally.

Your place or mine?
He's passionate and romantic, but not at the expense of his politeness and gallantry. He will rarely have sex with a woman on the first date. There are several reasons for this: first, feelings become involved in everything he does, including sex. He doesn't want to waste his sensitivity on a one-night stand. Another reason is that in order to fully appreciate the sensuality, he needs to know the woman he is making love to.

Checklist, before you dash out to meet him:
Look neat and tidy
(hint: no chipped nail varnish)
Don't have work or appointments later
(hint: be relaxed; no stress)
Leave your apartment clean and organised
(hint: in case he joins you home)
Bring a small casual gift (e.g. homemade candy)
(hint: show you made an effort)
Be brushed up on books, movies and TV shows
(hint: be interesting)

Tip: Never act insensitive around this guy. Don't make fun of him, even if you're just pulling his leg. He will take these statements to heart. A silly comment could actually ruin the entire evening.

CHAPTER 1

PREPARE YOURSELF

Catch his eye, capture his attention
Top 10 attention grabbers

1. Spark his interest with a playful look.
2. Be sparkling and outgoing.
3. Make sure your personality radiates positivity.
4. Wear an outfit that emphasises your femininity – but nothing vulgar.
5. Wear a bright smile.
6. Show a genuine interest in him and his world.
7. Admire him, but make it intelligent and specific – not just a general 'wow'.
8. Be very neat: your eyebrows, nails and make-up should be flawless.
9. Have a good sense of humour. It will be a big plus if you can praise yourself with humour.
10. Be intelligent and ask for his opinion.

The SHE. The woman!

It takes a special woman to hold onto this man. It's not enough to be feminine and positive – she must also be strong enough to handle his moodiness. She must be flexible in her ways. She must be loyal. She must strive to fill the days with harmony. Charming, humble, supportive and smart … it's no easy task, but it's worth it.

The Essence of her
Feminine – sparkling – compassionate – patient – flexible – harmonious –intelligent – warm – caring – down-to-earth – has a positive attitude – radiates joy and happiness – allows her man to be a man – entertaining – inspiring – supportive – pays attentive to detail – trustworthy – loyal – outgoing and charming –reassuring –gentle – humorous – shows her feelings

Cancer arousal meter
From 0 to 100… In three hours or more. Throwing yourself at him will seldom spark his erotic interest. Give him time to loosen up.

Remember: Be true to yourself
It doesn't matter if he is the most stunning guy you've ever met – if you don't match, you don't match. You may be able to put on a show for a while to hold his attention, but what's the point? We can't please everybody. We all have different needs, dreams, tastes and preferences. There's no such thing as a one-size-fits-all lover. Be yourself, and be true to who you are – always!

Very important: Show interest and admiration for him, but allow him to take the initiative. Never throw yourself at him.

CHAPTER 2

THE FIRST DATE

Getting your foot in the door
The basics

Support. This guy may be looking for a woman to fill the gaps in his life – whatever he feels he's missing. He's seeking someone supportive and loyal who he can trust.

Good vibes. She must also be able to add sunshine and harmony to his life. It's important that you radiate optimism, enthusiasm and positivity. A woman who helps him relax and feel good will always have an advantage.

Sharp, smart and sensitive. Inner beauty and intellectual qualities mean a lot to him. Inspire him with intelligent questions. Show him that you have an independent mind.

No mysteries. Avoid anything that will make him feel insecure about you. Evasiveness and mystery won't work with this guy. Be genuine and be direct – without being blunt or aggressive. Don't play hard to get. If you want to see him again, let him know – but do it in a feminine way.

Ease into him. Never make him feel cornered. Finding the right balance is a challenge. But if you really get along, you'll develop a sense of what to do and when. Give him space.

Whatever you do...

- **DON'T** be vulgar in any way.

- **DON'T** criticise his moodiness or sensitivity.

- **DON'T** flirt with other men.

- **DON'T** neglect yourself. Be healthy and look after your body.

- **DON'T** take his attention for granted.

Remember, this man needs reassurance. Don't be afraid to show him how you feel –

- **DON'T** be afraid to speak your mind, but avoid being argumentative.

- **DON'T** focus on the negative components of life. Be positive.

- **DON'T** keep him in the dark about your intentions.

- **DON'T** be sexually aggressive – or aggressive in at all.

- **DON'T** be ignorant. Show him that you have an alert mind.

but be careful and don't be too blunt and direct about it.

Signs you're in - or not

It's not always easy to figure out what's on a Cancer man's mind. He is an expert at protecting his feelings, and he won't reveal anything before he's confident in the relationship. He wants to save you – and himself! – from disappointment. Before this point, he'll probably be a little back and forth, careful not to commit to anything. If you really like him, be patient. Show your charisma and give him time and space to figure things out. When he does, the signals will be clear:

Chances are he will...

- show signs of kindness, like bringing you a little something he thinks you might need or like; it will be something personal
- be attentive and respond to you quickly
- light with happiness up when he sees you
- lose track of time when the two of you are talking
- show interest in your family
- open up about personal matters

Not your type? Making an exit

Let's hope you never find yourself needing to force a break-up with a Cancer. It will be devastating, no matter how down-to-earth you might be. He is sensitive, so any negativity from someone he cares about will upset him. He will usually take the hint quickly. Well, that's not exactly true. If you're being harsh, he will decide you don't live up to his expectations – and he'll think the break-up was his choice. Although he's loyal by nature, he has very little tolerance for ignorant or inconsiderate women.

There are exceptions to this rule, however rare. If you have managed to mesmerise him with your personality, you may need to apply blunter methods. Make sure a break-up is what you want before you take action!

Foolproof exit measures:

There will be no looking back after this. He will completely rule you out of his life. The measures are rough, so be gentle.

- Take him for granted
- Be cold, insensitive and unapproachable
- Insist on making your sex life more exciting by introducing porn and leather toys
- Criticise him for being weak and clingy if he wants to snuggle up
- Let yourself go. Gain weight. Stop visiting the hairdresser
- Introduce vulgarity in to your life: bad language, tacky clothes, etc.

CHAPTER 3

SEX'N STUFF

Seductive moves:
How to get him in the mood:

For a Cancer male, erotic advances must be gentle and subtle. Stuff that may turn on other men can have the opposite effect on him. Aggressiveness and assertiveness will push him away. Instead, try communicating with a smile and a long glance. Follow up with a gentle touch along his arm and over his fingers – and then a gentle kiss...

Preferences and erotic nature

During sex, he is passionate, strong and protective. He cares deeply about his partner's pleasure and enjoys guiding his woman through the mysteries of sex. He will be more than happy to introduce you to new ideas, but he'll always be careful not to push you. Sex with him is never boring and always fulfilling. He has a traditional streak, but he may surprise you by suggesting sex when you least expect it. He's not tied to the bedroom, but he'll never have sex in public places or in situations where you risk being caught. His amazing memory makes him a very exciting and understanding lover. He applies his memory of your previous encounters to make you feel like an erotic princess. He is truly a dream.

Hitting the right buttons

Although every sign has areas that are more sensitive than others, individual sensitivity may vary quite a bit. Don't go body-blind. Honing in on these erogenous zones and forgetting the rest of him is not a good idea. Use his erogenous zones to create sparks while turning him on, and as a passion booster when it gets heated. Watch his body language – including the most obvious of signs! Open your mind to the sensuality of touch and taste.

Key areas
His chest and nipples

Get it on
The Cancer man has two major 'on' buttons. The first are his nipples, which are very sensitive and respond well to soft touches, gentle rubbing, smooth lips or a playful tongue. The second is kissing, which appeals to his sensitivity and emotions – and this can also get him going.

Arouse him
Bring out your own sensitivity! Kiss him super gently, and take things from there. Never rush things. Let the feelings develop naturally. Caress him carefully and press yourself gently against his. Allow the kiss to become something that involves his entire body.

Surprise him

Take the initiative to be close to him. When you're out in public, press yourself against him – but only if the situation allows it; avoid tacky or clingy behaviour. A sensitive backrub when he least expects it can quickly turn into something more erotic, provided you are patient, gentle and sensitive about it.

Spice it up

The Cancer man is receptive to gentle touches. Keep this in mind, and have a play with oils, creams ... and maybe a little ice cream around his nipples.

Remember: Reassurance is important to him. Communicate your pleasure through voice and body.

His expectations

Sensual guidance. He expects his partner to encourage him in bed, but in a subtle and sensual way.

No constructive criticism! His woman must be careful not to criticise him in bed. That will have the same effect as throwing a bucket of ice in his face.

Seize the moment and enjoy. Take things slow. Enjoy the journey, and don't rush to reach climax.

Connect through intimacy. A long foreplay is very important to him. It feels good physically and enables him to connect emotionally.

Not just a physical thing. He experience erotic feelings on many levels. Everything is part of the bigger picture.

The tender touch. His partner must be sensitive and good at expressing her feelings through gentle touch, whispers and kissing.

Soft sensuality. Feminine underwear can be a great turn-on for this man – he likes anything that emphasises a woman's curves and femininity.

Your sensual preferences
Quiz yourself and find out whether this man is for you.

Where on the scale are you?
1 = Don't agree | 3 = Sure | 5 = Agree!

1. Kissing is an important part of sex and sensuality.
One a scale for 1 to 5, you are: 1 - 2 - 3- 4 - 5

2. Quiet intimacy can be more arousing than intense passion.
One a scale for 1 to 5, you are: 1 - 2 - 3- 4 - 5

3. The enjoyment of sex is not limited to physicality.
One a scale for 1 to 5, you are: 1 - 2 - 3- 4 - 5

4. Sensuality is a great way to express feelings.
One a scale for 1 to 5, you are: 1 - 2 - 3- 4 - 5

Score 15–20: Oh, wow … this is the stuff that sensual dreams are made of.
10 - 14: You share some important values and are able to inspire each other. It's a good start!
5 - 9: This is possible, but it'll take effort and mutual understanding to make it work.
1 - 4: You'll need to communicate and make some adjustments to achieve a fulfilling sex life.

CHAPTER 4

GENERAL STUFF

The big picture

Keep in mind that the characteristics of a Cancer may vary quite a bit depending on where within the sign he was born, as well as a wide range of additional astrological factors. But for now, let's stick to the basics. Just remember: don't jump to conclusions as soon as you meet him. Give him room to shine. Get to know the man behind the sign.

His personality: Pros and cons

Pros
- Romantic
- Sensitive
- Masculine
- Assertive
- Kind
- Intelligent
- A good listener
- Big-hearted
- Patient
- Sympathetic
- Ambitious
- Attentive
- Has a good memory
- A loyal friend

Cons
- Moody
- Jealous
- Self-obsessed
- Guarded and reserved
- Insecure
- Afraid of romantic failure
- Easily hurt
- Overly sensitive
- Demanding
- Judgmental
- Sulky
- Withdrawn
- Indecisive
- Easily influenced

Tip: How to show romantic interest

This is a perceptive guy – and that's why you have to be careful not to give him the wrong idea. Make sure that whatever you do has a personal touch and shows that you've been thinking about him: a special gift; a show or concert. Be thoughtful and make it personal.

Romantic Vibes

Mr Cancer:
The sensitive and masculine partner

The essence

Popular guy. It doesn't take much for him to become interested in someone. Since he's committed to finding the woman of his dreams, he may date quite a few.

Committed. It may take a while, but when he does commit to a relationship, he will very seldom stray. The essence of his world is love – but he's particular, and his partner must live up to his physical and mental expectations.

Loyal. He is very loyal to his old friends. If a new date doesn't approve of them, he will choose his friends over her – no matter how fascinated he might be.

No party-animal. The right woman doesn't have to worry. This man won't spend the whole night partying with the guys. In fact, he won't take a break from her very often. She is his source of love and inspiration, so why risk upsetting her?

Cherish the love. He must feel loved in order to thrive in a relationship. Fights, irritability, criticism, and sarcastic remarks will make him rethink the relationship no matter how strong his feelings might be.

The Sensitive and loving Alpha Male. Although he is sensitive, warm and caring, he still sees himself as The Man who makes the decisions.

Tip: How to show erotic interest

His sensuality is linked to his feelings. If you have reached a certain level of emotional connection with him, try gentle kisses.

Erotic Vibrations

Mr Cancer:
The romantic and strong lover

The essence

Seductive magic. He has the ability of seducing you without you even noticing. He is so subtle and sensitive, that you'll melt in his arms without thinking about it.

The fire within. He is one of the most romantic men in the zodiac – both in bed and out. However, sex with him is no sweet and innocent encounter. The right woman will bring out the masculinity and passion in him, and the sex will be intense with and beautiful.

True essence of sensuality. Sex with him is intense and beautiful. There will be no vulgarities. No dirty language. No silly or rude suggestions. He is a true sensual lover.

Master of erotic memory. His memory is excellent, and he'll remember your preferences and build on his knowledge as he goes.

Be sassy, but keep it feminine. He doesn't mind you taking the initiative and being creative, but remember no to overdo it. He wants his woman to be feminine in every aspect of life – including in the bedroom.

An erotic dream. He won't mind teaching you a thing or two in bed, but he will do so very gently: a few whispers in your ear while he guides you.

CHAPTER 5

COMPATIBILITY QUIZ

_____

Are you banging your head against the wall, or does he unleash your positive potential? Do you provoke him or bring out the best in him? Does he make you throw your arms up in exasperation, or do you feel inspired and complete in his company? Are the two of you headed towards doom or dream? Take the test to find out.

Question 1.
Do you always tell your partner about your erotic needs and preferences?

A. Yes, of course.
B. Rarely. My partner is very sensitive. Anything more adventurous than the missionary position would probably offend him.
C. Sometimes, but it depends on my mood ... and how sassy my ideas are!

Question 2.
Do you tend to criticize your partner if there's something you're unhappy with?

A. Yes. How else am I supposed to get my point through to him?
B. No. If you approach someone with negativity, you'll get negativity in return. I try to be diplomatic.
C. Sometimes, but only if I'm in a bad mood

(cont.)

Question 3.
What comes to mind when you hear the word "sex"?

A. Romance, a sensual setting and pleasure.
B. Joy, passion and satisfaction.
C. Spontaneity, intensity and hot energy.

Question 4.
How do you deal with moodiness?

A. I know it's important to be flexible and understanding, but frequent moodiness drives me nuts.
B. I have very little tolerance for moodiness. It's insensitive to bother other people with your mood swings.
C. There is usually a reason my partner is feeling how he is. If he's low, I try to make him feel better.

Question 5.
Do you find it easy to forgive?

A. No. If someone has hurt me, the anger stays with me for a long time.
B. Forgiveness isn't easy, but I do try my best.
C. If someone asks for forgiveness, it means they have realised that their actions were wrong. The least you can do is forgive them.

Question 6.
How would you react if someone made a joke on your guy's behalf?

A. It'd be okay. We shouldn't take ourselves too seriously.
B. I'd never tolerate that. I always stick up for my guy, whether he's there or not.
C. I would probably hit back with a joke of my own, aimed at her guy.

Question 7.
How do you feel about a guy who takes command when the going gets tough?

A. I really appreciate a strong man I can rely on, providing he doesn't run me over...
B. Pure bliss! He would be my dream man!
C. I've never really been in to macho stuff. Guys like that bore me.

Question 8.
Do you find it easy to express your feelings?

A. It's so important to show how you feel. It removes insecurities and makes?
B. Yes, but sometimes I forget...
C. My guy knows that I love him. There's no need to remind him every day.

Question 9.
How do you feel about kissing?

A. I love it. I could never be in a relationship without kisses. So many feelings are expressed through kissing.
B. No big deal. A kiss is a kiss, right?
C. Kissing is a great way to share closeness and intimacy.

Question 10.
Do you ever tell your partner about previous lovers?

A. Sure. It's part of my past and who I am. Why shouldn't I?
B. Very seldom, and only if I feel I have to.
C. Never, that would be very insensitive.

SCORE	A	B	C
Question 1	10	1	5
Question 2	1	10	5
Question 3	10	5	1
Question 4	5	1	10
Question 5	1	5	10
Question 6	1	10	5
Question 7	5	10	1
Question 8	10	5	1
Question 9	10	1	5
Question 10	1	5	10

75 – 100
Love, sensitivity and harmony have descended upon every area of your life, and it seems to have happened effortlessly and naturally. Your man is masculine and strong – as well as soft and sensitive. There's no either-or; he is everything, and he's the perfect man for you! This relationship promises to be amazing. You know how to handle him when he withdraws into himself. You don't get hurt if he seems distant and stressed, because you know this is his way of dealing with life. Love, respect, understanding and consideration form the foundation of this relationship – which probably will last for quite some time.

51 – 74
Yes, he will probably make your eyes twinkle. And yes, he will sometimes be a challenge! Moodiness is a part of this masculine man, but don't take it personally. He has a lot going on in his mind, and sometimes he just withdraws. Ironically, his sensitivity is exactly the thing that can make him insensitive at times. But you've been looking for a real man, and here he is. He can make your knees turn to jelly, and his romantic streak and sensitivity make him incredibly loveable. Although there might be a few ups and downs, see it through. He's worth it.

26 – 50
There are moments with him that are pure bliss – moments when you're sure you've met the most wonderful man in the world. However, sometimes, when you look into his eyes, you notice a strange seriousness. It's something you can't put your finger on, and he doesn't want to talk about everything – but he expects you to understand. If you don't, he'll be confused. This is part of why it may be difficult to establish complete harmony. Maybe you're too restless for him. Maybe you need more fire and energy in your life. The two of you have different ways of communicating, and sometimes you talk and walk right past each other. It's up to you whether you should keep walking...

10 – 25
How the two of you got together in the first place is a mystery. You were probably attracted to his masculinity and assertiveness. Or maybe it was a classic case of 'opposites attract'? Whatever the spark, it probably won't stay alight very long. His moodiness and sensitivity drive you nuts; meanwhile, he regards you as blunt and distant. This relationship requires a lot of work. It's possible, but is it worth it? Right now, you're probably just annoying each other. Both of you will could find a better match elsewhere. Change course and pursue true happiness and joy.

Thoughts...
Remember, moods can play tricks with your feelings. Don't make rushed decisions. Take a deep breath and think again...

LEO the male

YOUR DATE: LEO
23 July–22 August

The Essence of him

Impossible to ignore – confident – generous – social – enthusiastic – positive – big-hearted – has a big personality – energetic and lively – engaging – encouraging – masculine – boyish – playful – loves being the centre of attention – loyal – reliable – flashy – careless with money – attentive – kind – agreeable – friendly – understanding – superficial – temperamental – naturally authoritative

...and remember: Don't forget to show your interest in him by asking questions and expressing admiration for who he is and what he's done.

Blind Date – speedy essentials

Who's waiting for you?
Forget about shy and modest guys with sweaty palms and nervous glances. This guy will leap up from his chair and greet you with a charismatic smile. He will look you in the eye and not be afraid to establish physical contact with you right away. He will be genuinely pleased to see you. The Leo man radiates enthusiasm, and it may almost seem like his entire body is smiling. If the first impression is right and the two of you click, then you're in for a very exciting evening – and his body language will give this away. All said, this is a man who is capable of sweeping you off your feet in minutes.

Emergency fixes for embarrassing pauses
A quiet Leo? He must be suffering from the flu with a high fever. Being quiet is against his nature. He is outgoing and enthusiastic, and embarrassing pauses simply do not exist in his world – or at least, they're extremely rare. Although talking and socialising come easily to him, he won't mind you taking the initiative. Just make sure to be positive. Avoid bringing up bad news.

Your place or mine?
If you ask a Leo, life is for living, loving – and lusting. Why wait until later? If the two of you hit it off and feel the erotic temperature rising, then he won't need much encouragement to take the next step. The more he likes you, the better the chance that he'll suggest a coffee at his place – or yours. This guy has no inhibitions.

Checklist, before you dash out to meet him:
Be on time
(hint: Don't be stressed)
Wear modest, feminine make-up
(hint: Not too much. Keep it classy)
Rinse your mouth and floss your teeth
(hint: Flash a beautiful and fresh smile)
Wear a designer item or something a little luxurious
(hint: He enjoys the finer things in life)
Brush up on positive news
(hint: Keep an optimistic approach)

Tip: If he really likes you, he will pamper you. Never undercut his generosity with comments like: 'That's too much' or 'That's too expensive'. Be happy. Be positive. Be grateful!

CHAPTER 1

PREPARE YOURSELF

Catch his eye, capture his attention
Top 10 attention grabbers

1. Allow yourself to be admired by men, and respond with a smile.
2. Be stylish and show off a hint of luxury.
3. Carry yourself with femininity and grace.
4. Flatter him in public.
5. Let him know you admire him.
6. Put a positive spin on everything.
7. Be sparkling and happy – and show off a genuine smile.
8. Take the initiative to suggest something fun or unusual to do.
9. Wear something expensive.
10. Impress him with something you've done, but don't outshine him.

The SHE. The woman!

He needs a woman who can shine by his side – a jewel to make him look good. In return, he will treat her like a queen. She must be stylish, attractive and feminine, and know a little about a lot of things. He wants someone smart, but she doesn't need to have a doctorate; although he is confident, he can actually feel uncomfortable in the company of a woman he suspects is smarter than he is. His ideal woman must appreciate his masculinity and express her affection clearly. Praising and flattering him is also very important.

The Essence of her

Stylish – attractive – feminine – entertaining – smart, without being too intellectual – up-to-date on current affairs – attentive – has a positive outlook – generous – enjoys the pleasures of life – supportive and loyal - adventurous and playful – sensual, with a fondness for sex – vocal in her admiration- productive and constructive

---

Leo arousal meter

From 0 to 100... In less than 10 minutes – or it could be a week. It depends on the encouragement he gets. The good thing is, it's up to you…

Remember: Be true to yourself
It doesn't matter if he is the most stunning guy you've ever met – if you don't match, you don't match. You may be able to put on a show for a while to hold his attention, but what's the point? We can't please everybody. We all have different needs, dreams, tastes and preferences. There's no such thing as a one-size-fits-all lover. Be yourself, and be true to who you are – always!

Very important: Be charming and outgoing, but never steal his spotlight. If he feels like he is standing in your shadow, it won't take him long to head off to find a place where he can shine.

CHAPTER 2

THE FIRST DATE

Getting your foot in the door
The basics

You don't have to be a model... but make sure you look good. Emphasise your feminine features.

Be interesting. Let him know that you have a fondness for everything new and exciting – without coming across as a trend-follower.

Flatter him. Look into his eyes and tell him he's the best-looking guy you've met in a long time. This won't scare him off. He'll love the praise.

Look at the bright side. Humour is important if you want to capture him. Make him laugh and focus on the sunny sides of life.

Be generous. After you've seen him a couple of times, buy him a gift. Make sure it has luxury written all over it. It doesn't have to be big – just let him know you appreciate nice things.

A little competition... Let him see you surrounded by attentive males. This strategy never fails. Mr Leo is eager to capture a woman who is popular with other men.

Whatever you do...

- **DON'T** boss him around.

- **DON'T** try to outsmart him or point out his mistakes.

- **DON'T** talk about ex-boyfriends.

- **DON'T** wear anything too suggestive.

- **DON'T** make jokes on his behalf, even innocent ones.

Remember,
There's no need to feel shy about his generosity. If he really likes you, he will love

- **DON'T** suggest that something he bought for you might be too expensive.

- **DON'T** be negative.

- **DON'T** suggest splitting the bill.

- **DON'T** agree with him just for the sake of it.

- **DON'T** play games or tease him, no matter how innocently.

spoiling you. Just remember to let him know how grateful you are.

Signs you're in - or not

If a Leo man likes you, you'll know! He's simple in this regard: either he likes you or he doesn't. He doesn't need to think about it forever. If it feels right, he'll go for it. If it's not working out, he'll deal with it. Either way, he won't waste time. If he's into you, there will be no evasive hints or modest gifts. He won't give you a single rose. He'll give you a dozen. He won't just invite you out for pizza; he'll dance with you under the stars. Still not sure? Here are some ways to tell that Mr Leo is smitten:

Chances are he will...

- give you a gift or a little surprise
- pop by – not to check on you, but just to say hi
- show you off to his friends
- call to make sure you made it home safely
- suggest going away together
- show genuine interest in what you're up to

Not your type? Making an exit

This man will never stay in a relationship with a woman who has turned into a grey cloud over his life. He needs happiness and positivity to grow and flourish, and he can't do this without optimism and energy. He wants a partner who shines and makes the days happy and bright. If you fail to meet his expectations, chances are he'll be the one getting rid of you. He loves women. This is a popular guy, and he won't have any trouble moving on.

If you are getting tired of the whole thing, but Mr Leo is still around, you've obviously managed to charm him deeply. He probably sees a side to you that he finds exciting. Or maybe you're a jewel he likes to show off out in public. In that case, it's time to show him your less-appealing side...

Foolproof exit measures:

If you go ahead with these suggestions, you will come across as mean, cynical and cold. There will be no turning back from this.

- Criticise his spending, even if he has spent the money on you
- Accuse him of living in a fantasy world
- Never offer any praise or approval
- Let yourself go. Be indifferent about your looks
- Interrupt him and argue with him constantly – in public as well
- Tell him to stop being so childish and to behave like a man

CHAPTER 3

SEX'N STUFF

Seductive moves:
How to get him in the mood:

Admiring his body is a good start. Don't forget his 'toolbox'. He's very proud of his equipment, regardless of size. If you show sensual admiration while the two of you are out on the town, he will probably turn into a wonderful and passionate stud as soon as you are back home.

Preferences and erotic nature

Remember to let him know how much you enjoy … well, everything: him, his body, his lovemaking – the lot. Don't leave it until later. Show your pleasure in bed with words, sighs and touches. This will fuel his passion and keep him going. He's not an adventurous lover, and he's happy with traditional stuff. Never criticise him or ask him to change his ways. If you want to try something new, present it as an exciting suggestion. Don't push him if he doesn't seem eager. When the time has come to sleep, never turn your back on him. Take time to cuddle and praise him. If you forget to do this, he will probably start sulking.

Hitting the right buttons

Although every sign has areas on the body that are more sensitive than others, individual sensitivity may vary quite a bit. Don't go body-blind. Honing in on these erogenous zones and forgetting the rest of him is not a good idea. Use these areas to create sparks while turning him on, and as a passion-booster when things get heated. Watch his body language – including the most obvious of signs. Open your mind to the sensuality of touch and taste.

Key area
His back

Get it on
If you give him an innocent back massage, you could be in for a passionate response. The lighter the touch, the heavier the breathing. If you're not in the mood for sex, make sure the pressure is firm.

Arouse him
Be gentle. Let the tips of your fingers gently play over his bare back. Soft lips and a playful tongue will make his heart beat faster. Rubbing his back with a towel as he gets out of the shower will usually evolve into something more passionate. When out in public, there are endless ways to arouse him without drawing attention. An innocent hug could turn into a very intimate and sensual moment – and be a good reason to quickly hail a taxi back home.

Surprise him
Give him a flirtatious call during the day. There's no need to be blunt; he's got a pretty good imagination. Suggest meeting up later that evening…

Spice it up
The 'helpless female' act is a great turn-on for this guy, as it gives him a chance to show off his masculine side. Oh, and sassy feminine underwear is a plus.

Remember: Never, ever, give the impression that you're up for an erotic encounter just to measure his interest. This can cause him to lose trust in you, and change the way he feels about you.

His expectations

Hot'n spicy. Sex is an important part of his life. He takes passion seriously.

No mixed signals. Avoid playful teasing. Other guys may be turned on by it. This guy will be offended.

Be vocal. Verbal affirmations turn him on, both inside and outside the bedroom. He loves, and needs, to be stimulated with words. A woman who tells him how much she admires him as a lover and praises his body – and how he uses it – will always have a special place in his heart.

No lazy chicks! He needs a woman who is active in bed. A passive partner can shift his mood from steamy to chilly in no time.

A little bit of everything. His ideal partner will be feminine, playful and passionate.

Your sensual preferences
Quiz yourself and find out whether this man is for you.

Where on the scale are you?
1 = Don't agree | 3 = Sure | 5 = Agree!

1. Hot and exciting sex requires a man to be passionate and dominant in bed.
One a scale for 1 to 5, you are : 1 - 2 - 3- 4 - 5

2. Expressing pleasure during sex is very important.
One a scale for 1 to 5, you are : 1 - 2 - 3- 4 - 5

3. There is no need for drawn-out foreplay in order to experience passion and pleasure.
One a scale for 1 to 5, you are : 1 - 2 - 3- 4 - 5

4. Passion and erotic impulsiveness are far more important than gadgets and new positions.
One a scale for 1 to 5, you are : 1 - 2 - 3- 4 - 5

Score 15–20: You have the capacity to thoroughly enjoy exploring each other passionately – and frequently.
Score 10–14: There will be loads of passion and very few slow moments. Just remember to convey your feelings of pleasure clearly.
Score 5–9: As long as you give him the encouragement he needs, both verbally and physically, he will do his best to please you.
Score 1–4: This guy may be a little too passionate and direct for you at times. Don't tell him to slow down while you're in the middle of things. Tell him about your preferences before having sex. If you do it seductively, he will remember.

CHAPTER 4

GENERAL STUFF

The big picture

Keep in mind that the characteristics of a Leo may vary quite a bit depending on where within the sign he was born, as well as a wide range of additional astrological factors. But for now, let's stick to the basics. Just remember: don't jump to conclusions as soon as you meet him. Give him room to shine. Get to know the man behind the sign.

His personality: Pros and cons

Pros
- Generous
- Has a positive outlook on life
- Enthusiastic
- Confident
- Lives in the moment
- Has a big personality
- Masculine
- Playful and boyish
- Encouraging
- Entertaining
- Loyal
- Honest
- Trustworthy
- Stylish

Cons
- Childish
- Careless with money
- Blunt
- Temperamental
- Stubborn
- Ambitious, even ruthless
- Selfish
- Demanding of attention
- Impressed by status and wealth
- Easily offended
- Takes himself too seriously
- Unable to tolerate criticism
- Self-centered
- Snobbish

Tip: How to show romantic interest

Express admiration and treat him to little luxuries, like a special wine or a beer, cashmere socks, etc. Make sure he knows you've made an effort.

Romantic Vibes

Mr Leo:
The protective and generous partner

The essence

Royal treatment. The Leo man will pamper and spoil his woman in every way. He will treat her like a like a queen. There is only one small catch ... she must accept him as the king.

Embrace his manliness. A woman who can handle his masculinity will reap the rewards of his generosity and attentiveness.

My woman! He loves showing off an attractive partner, but he doesn't like competition and can become jealous if you receive too much attention from other guys when you're out. The same applies to male friends and former boyfriends.

Reliable. He is very loyal and will come rushing whenever you need help or guidance.

Genuinely positive and optimistic. Although he may seem to have everything under control, some Leos are just keeping their fingers crossed and hoping for the best. This has nothing to do with laziness; he just genuinely believes that everything will be fine. But you don't need to worry. He has a unique gift of landing on his feet.

Tip: How to show erotic interest

Whisper erotic suggestions into his ear, but don't be crude about it. Emphasise his strength and qualities as a lover, and tell him how much you are looking forward to feeling him...

Erotic Vibrations

Mr Leo:
The powerful and positive lover

The essence

Enthusiasm. It's impossible to be indifferent about sex while dating a Leo. He is just as enthusiastic about sex as he is about everything else in life, and it's infectious. If your ideal lover is quiet, gentle and sensitive, you may find him a little overwhelming.

Don't hold back. Passion is his middle name, and he expects his partner to be just as excited. But don't worry – he won't turn sex into an exhausting marathon. He knows when he needs to take it easy.

Great lover. A Leo takes great pride in pleasing his partner, and he seldom fails. One hint is all it takes, and he'll be ready to prove himself as the world's greatest lover.

Knows his way around. There will be no insecure fumbling under the covers. This guy knows what he's doing, and he's usually pretty good at it. He is straight to the point and can go for hours without getting bored or tired.

No games! Whatever you do, never tease him. This guy doesn't enjoy playing games! If you have accepted an intimate invitation from him, you'd better finish what you started.

When he's hot, he's hot. This guy doesn't waste time. He will probably sweep you off your feet sooner than you think…

CHAPTER 5

COMPATIBILITY QUIZ

Are you banging your head against the wall, or does he unleash your positive potential? Do you provoke him or bring out the best in him? Does he make you throw your arms up in exasperation, or do you feel inspired and complete in his company? Are the two of you headed towards doom or dream? Take the test to find out.

Question 1.
Your man enthusiastically tells you about an project he's about to start working on. What's your reaction?

A. I'd say, 'Wow, great!' I don't want to ruin his enthusiasm, even though I know he tends to lose interest if things don't meet his expectations.
B. I'd probably ask him if he had given it enough thought. I've heard the same story many times before.
C. I'd share his enthusiasm – of course. I love positive men!

Question 2.
You've just finished a romantic dinner when he looks at you passionately and says: 'Come and join me in the jungle!' How do you respond?

A. With excitement.
B. I'd quite like that – even though his erotic invitations can be a little unrefined at times…
C. Sigh. I'm so tired of his macho stuff. I'd have told him to help me clear the table instead

(cont.)

Question 3.
Do you think it's OK for you partner to try and impress other women?

A. No, not at all. Whenever he tries to convince the world that he's Mr Wonderful, I feel completely ignored.
B. It's no problem for me. He is who he is, and I'm proud of him.
C. It's OK, provided he doesn't overdo it.

Question 4.
Do you get nervous when your checking account balance gets low?

A. It depends how many bills I have lying around.
B. Of course! I don't print new money in the kitchen.
C. I'm pretty relaxed about it. If I have spent a little too much one month, I'll save a little extra the next.

Question 5.
Have you ever cuddled up with your man, aroused him ... and then rolled over to sleep?

A. Never! That's mean and insensitive!
B. I did once, for fun ... but he didn't like that.
C. Sure. I love teasing my partner.

Question 6.
How do you deal with your partner if he suddenly gets quiet and withdraws into himself?

A. Everyone needs a little space sometimes. I leave him alone and make sure he knows I'm there if he needs me.
B. Nothing much. He can get a little grumpy, but I don't know why he always has to take it out on me.
C. There's only one thing to do: I am sweet and gentle to him.

Question 7.
Do you express pleasure clearly when having sex?

A. Not really; I'm not all that passionate.
B. Absolutely. It's impossible not to – my partner is hot.
C. Depends on my mood. Sometimes I like to take it slow and easy.

Question 8.
How would you define excitement?

A. Streaming an action movie.
B. Everyday surprises, sensuality and love.
C. Days without routine, a spontaneous sex life, travel and new experiences – big and small.

Question 9.
Do you think it's important to flatter your partner's body in bed?

A. Sometimes, but only if it feels natural to do so.
B. Yes, absolutely – both with words and touches.
C. I've never really thought about it.

Question 10.
How do you feel about sex that is intensely passionate from the very first second?

A. It's wonderful – once in a while.
B. I love it. Passion makes me feel alive.
C. Not my favourite. I'm not into sexual gymnastics.

SCORE	A	B	C
Question 1	10	5	1
Question 2	5	1	10
Question 3	1	10	5
Question 4	5	1	10
Question 5	10	5	1
Question 6	10	1	5
Question 7	1	10	5
Question 8	1	5	10
Question 9	5	10	1
Question 10	5	10	1

75 – 100

The most perfect, attractive and exciting man could walk into your life tomorrow – and you would ignore him. You have already found the man who can transform any rainy day into an exciting adventure. You know how important it is to encourage people around you, including your Leo. You make the sun shine for him, and he rewards you by pampering you in every way possible. Your sexual chemistry is strong, and you are simply hooked on each other. Passion flows naturally and freely ... wow. Full steam ahead!

51 – 74

You understand the importance of compliments: without reassurance and positive input, life can become lethargic and uninspiring. You are the kind of woman who helps this man open up and enjoy life. Remember that the Leo needs to establish himself as the dominating male, but don't let this put you off. He has no urge to control you; he only wants to show you that he's capable of protecting and taking care of you – including in the bedroom. Sex is important to him. Although he may not appreciate that you're not as active as he is, he will respect your honesty and do whatever it takes to please you.

26 – 50

One thing is certain: this relationship will never be boring. In fact, sparks will fly quite frequently – sometimes positive sparks, sometimes negative. Avoid obvious bummers like stepping on his ego. Constructive criticism during sex is another no-no. He has zero tolerance for criticism in bed, and even helpful comments can turn him off completely. Show him love and admiration, and be the queen by his side. Don't deny him the odd moment of luxury from time to time – even though you may not be in the mood for splurging. Too much work? It will probably be trying at times, but if you like him, there aren't many options. He is kind, passionate and generous. He is also self-centered, childish and temperamental. If you feel his negative sides overshadows his positive ones, you may want to explore love elsewhere.

10 – 25

Some relationships are challenging. This one is basically just hard work. It doesn't matter if you mean well, or that you act out of care for him: fussing will get you nowhere. The only thing you'll achieve is putting him in a bad mood – and a miserable Leo is a pain. He feeds on admiration and love. If you deny him this, he will lose his sparkle – and eventually lose himself. He is careful not to let this happen, so if things aren't going well, he will probably be out of your life before you get a chance to kick him out. Happiness waits elsewhere – for both of you.

Thoughts...
Time, effort and love will determine whether this relationship is built to last. Embrace everything that feels good, and be constructive about the rest.

VIRGO the male

YOUR DATE: VIRGO
23 August – 22 September

The Essence of him

Intelligent – outgoing – charming – analytical – private – slightly split personality – strict perfectionist – thorough – down to earth – self-disciplined – workaholic – interesting – knowledgeable – health conscious – lone wolf – moody – temperamental – kind – assertive – polite – attentive – entertaining – helpful – loyal – considerate – practical – has a distinctive boyish nature, he'll never grow old

...and remember: Although he may come across as confident and outgoing, he can actually be a little shy when it comes to women. Go ahead and take the initiative, but be classy about it.

Blind Date – speedy essentials

Who's waiting for you?
He may try to be cool about it, but he'll be looking at his watch and towards the entrance. The anticipation can make him a little nervous, but don't be fooled, he's got everything under control. He has sorted out the dining options or whatever you've planned to do. He won't change his mind or pull out if he discovers that you're not his type. He'll see it through and make you feel comfortable in his company. This is a stylish guy. He's neat with a keen eye for detail – which means he'll be keeping an eye on your appearance too...!

Emergency fixes for embarrassing pauses
Although he usually drapes himself in self-confidence, he can get a little shy if you've managed to dazzle him with your sparkling laugh. Ask him about something and be smart about it. These guys usually know quite a bit about most things and they enjoy sharing the knowledge. If you manage to see everyday topics from new angles, then you won't have to worry about pauses.

Your place or mine?
Neither. If he's looking for a romantic relationship, he won't suggest having sex. An erotic invitation on the first date usually means he's more interested in your body than your mind and not a long term commitment. He's very patient. If he really likes you, he's prepared to get to know you and wait until he has met you two, three... or five, or seven times.

Checklist, before you dash out to meet him:
Hair in place, eyebrows fixed, well-kept hands
(hint: Be tidy)
Running on schedule
(hint: Don't be late)
Feeling good, no sniffles coming on
(hint: No germs)
Up to date on current affairs
(hint: Be alert)
Got some fun ideas and opinions
(hint: Be interesting)

Tip: NEVER hassle this guy. Fuss and high expectations can mess up work-relations and romantic feelings.

CHAPTER 1

PREPARE YOURSELF

Catch his eye, capture his attention
Top 10 attention grabbers

1. An alert mind and bright eyes.
2. Intelligent comments. Little sidekicks will make him pay attention.
3. Stylish and feminine clothing.
4. Sparkling playfulness - but no "dumb blonde".
5. Display a positive attitude towards others.
6. Ask for his opinion.
7. Display your sporty and healthy sides, but don't overdo it.
8. Emphasize the quality in you and everything you do.
9. Keep a positive outlook on life. Ease his mind if he seems stressed out.
10. Don't come on too strong. Make him feel relaxed in your company.

The SHE. The woman!

This man is extremely choosy. His dream date is intellectually alert – without threatening his professional authority. She is classy and good looking – without spending too much time in front of the mirror or wasting money on expensive creams, treatments and clothes. She is charming, sparkling and feminine – but never silly and giggling. Her outlook is down to earth, but still creative and independent. No wonder there are so many bachelors born under the sign of Virgo…

The Essence of her
Smart and intelligent – well informed and up to date on current affairs – tidy and well kept – independent – assertive without being pushy – feminine and classy – genuine – down to earth – interesting – not afraid of voicing her opinion or supporting unusual ideas – outgoing – disciplined – reliable and supportive – adaptable, without being easily led – organized – calm and collected when the world throws her a challenge

---

Virgo arousal meter
From 0 to 100… in several hours. This guy is not driven by intense passion. He's an explorer who takes it slow.

Remember: Be true to yourself
It doesn't matter if he is the most stunning guy you've ever met – if you don't match, you don't match. You may be able to put on a show for a while to hold his attention, but what's the point? We can't please everybody. We all have different needs, dreams, tastes and preferences. There's no such thing as a one-size-fits-all lover. Be yourself, and be true to who you are – always!

Very important: If you feel a cold coming on, call him and move the date to another day. DO NOT spend the evening sniffling around this guy!

CHAPTER 2

THE FIRST DATE

Getting your foot in the door
The basics

Be charming, stylish and almost a little dignified. Avoid anything that may give him the impression that you're easy.

Pay close attention to details. Apart from your outfit, make-up and hairstyle, your mind needs to be alert!

Humor is a big hit with these guys, but there's a difference between being humorous and being silly. Convey a bit of intelligence, you'll be scoring major points.

Inspire him. If you are good at something, let him know. If you can introduce him to a new interest, do so.

Show good taste. This does not only apply to food. It applies to everything! Quality matters very much for these people!

Look good. If he has invited you out, put on something feminine and elegant, and remember to show up on time.

Punctuality is very important when seducing this guy. He dislikes wasting time - and money - and having to wait will only put him in a bad mood.

Whatever you do...

- **DON'T** be late.

- **DON'T** look scruffy or wear too much makeup.

- **DON'T** ditch your manners.

- **DON'T** command the attention and interrupt him.

- **DON'T** sneeze and cough without be discreet about it.

Remember, give him space and time to figure things out.

- **DON'T** make silly jokes on behalf of others.

- **DON'T** throw your money around.

- **DON'T** criticize people who work long hours.

- **DON'T** talk about illnesses you have had or may have.

- **DON'T** give the impression that you don't know much about current affairs.

If you push him into making a decision, you may end up pushing him out of your life.

Signs you're in - or not

This can actually be a little tricky to determine. He is usually very charming and outgoing. However, that's no measure for his interest in you – at least not when it comes to romance. Never take anything for granted. A positive attitude may indicate that he finds you fun and interesting – as a friend.

The challenge with this guy is that he usually finds himself at a crossroad – friend, fun or lover. It may be difficult to interpret what goes on in his mind, but there are subtle signals which will indicate that you have sparked his fire:

Chances are he will...

- take the initiative to do something
- suggest getting together – privately
- splash out money on you
- suggest working out together
- ask for your opinion
- make you top priority, ahead of work and friends

Not your type? Making an exit

The Virgo has a very practical approach to these things. He doesn't waste his time on anything – or anyone. If things don't work out, he'll be off. Even though you feel you've made your best effort to come across as smart, intelligent and charming, this man is constantly analyzing you – without you even noticing. He'll be adding things together and creating his own perception of you, and he usually gets it spot on. If he thinks you won't be able to live up to his expectations, well, that's it for him. It's just a matter of finding his perfect mate – which isn't very easy...

However, there are slow movers. There are Virgos who may be too distracted by work or whatever to get the point. If his lack of spontaneity and joy is driving you nuts, if you're getting tired of his need for achievement, if you are craving romance and more passion in your life, you may need to push things in order for him to make a move.

Foolproof exit measures:

These suggestions may seem a little over the top, but if you're going to send him a message, you might as well do it thoroughly.

- Let yourself go. Skip waxing, manicures and hair appointments
- Criticize his analytical mind and accuse him of being hung up in details
- Blow all your money partying with friends
- Be late or forget about dates
- Talk about previous lovers and how good they were
- Make a mess in the kitchen, bathroom, living room... and leave it for him to tidy up

CHAPTER 3

SEX'N STUFF

Seductive moves:
How to get him in the mood:

Remember, you are dealing with a guy who'd rather flash his brain than his 'tool box'". Cheap hook-up lines and obvious seductive moves will do nothing but annoy him. This man regards sex as an aesthetic experience, and not a lesson in breath-taking gymnastics. In other words, be subtle.

Preferences and erotic nature

Many Virgos enjoy having sex in the shower. Apart from the fact that it feels good, it satisfies his need for cleanliness. Personal hygiene is important! An erotic suggestion when you return from the gym in your workout clothes is a no-no-no! However, let him sneak a peek while you're taking a shower, and he won't need much encouragement to take it from there.

He does have a liberal streak and is open to ideas, providing you don't go over the top. Introduce him to something new and suggest being a little more daring. Mr Virgo can be surprisingly passionate with the right encouragement. Although sex can be a great release for stress and bottled-up frustrations, make sure not to bother him when he's busy. Wait until he's ready for a 'time out'.

Hitting the right buttons

Although every sign has areas on the body that are more sensitive than others, individual sensitivity may vary quite a bit. Don't go body-blind. Honing in on these erogenous zones and forgetting the rest of him is not a good idea. Use these areas to create sparks while turning him on, and as a passion-booster when things get heated. Watch his body language – including the most obvious of signs. Open your mind to the sensuality of touch and taste.

Key areas
His midsection. Stomach and waist

Get it on
Don't poke around with his midsection unless you truly want to get intimate with him. His entire stomach area is particularly sensitive and usually brings out the passionate side of him (usually, because he is one of the most self-controlled guys in the zodiac.)

Arouse him
Your absolute best bet is to start working on his stomach area. Use very light touches when stroking him. He also loves having his tummy scratched with your fingernails – providing you do it carefully, of course. Don't forget to use your lips and tongue. Men born under this sign love the sensation of moist lips gently brushing his skin and a playful tongue running over the stomach. If the two of you are having a bath or a shower, make sure to caress his erogenous zone with soap and water.

Surprise him

Let's be realistic; this guy is far too disciplined to be easily surprised. Your best bet is to make it seem accidental. Allow him to sneak a peek at you when you're taking a shower. This is actually one of the things that can have a distracting – effect on him.

Spice it up

Play with taste and temperature. Apply a touch of ice cream to his tummy and gently enjoy it off him with your warm lips and tongue. Don't focus on just one spot. Use his entire midsection.

Remember: There are no shortcuts to his bed. He can't relax and focus on sex if he's got work on his mind, or if the apartment – or his partner – looks a mess.

His expectations

Communicate. You don't have to be a lioness in bed, you don't even have to be vocal, but make sure to express how you feel.

Be clear. Never leave him guessing.

All in, or out! This man never does things half way. If something is worth doing, it's worth doing well – an approach which applies to his erotic life as well.

Be vocal. He takes great pride in pleasing his woman and feedback is crucial. A quiet and non-expressive woman can make him feel insecure and turn him off completely.

Take the initiative. He doesn't mind a woman who takes the initiative in bed, providing she's playful and feminine.

No aggressiveness, please! Aggressive women turn him off, not only in bed but also in every other aspect of life.

Be creative. A creative partner can do wonders for his self-esteem. Sharing the responsibility while broadening his erotic horizons will make him relax and thoroughly enjoy the whole thing.

Guide him. Don't be afraid to guide him and drop a few hints. He'll appreciate it.

Your sensual preferences
Quiz yourself and find out whether this man is for you.

Where on the scale are you?
1 = Don't agree | 3 = Sure | 5 = Agree!

1. Communication is important during sex
One a scale for 1 to 5, you are: 1 - 2 - 3- 4 - 5

2. Creativity can make an erotic encounter more fulfilling
One a scale for 1 to 5, you are: 1 - 2 - 3- 4 - 5

3. Playfulness can bring out passion and sensuality in you
One a scale for 1 to 5, you are: 1 - 2 - 3- 4 - 5

4. Attention to personal hygiene is important before having sex
One a scale for 1 to 5, you are: 1 - 2 - 3- 4 - 5

Score 15–20: You share some of the essentials, which is a great base to build on.
Score 10–14: Your erotic differences can actually be an inspiration and make you grow.
Score 5–9: Never leave things to chance. Don't assume he knows what you want. Make sure your spontaneity doesn't make him feel obliged to perform.
Score 1–4: Make sure to communicate desires and expectations in order to avoid misunderstandings. An erotic chat before having sex could be a good idea.

CHAPTER 4

GENERAL STUFF

The big picture

Keep in mind that the characteristics of a Virgo may vary quite a bit depending on where within the sign he was born, as well as a wide range of additional astrological factors. But for now, let's stick to the basics. Just remember: don't jump to conclusions as soon as you meet him. Give him room to shine. Get to know the man behind the sign.

His personality: Pros and cons

Pros
- Focused
- Kind and generous
- Loyal and supportive
- Excellent sense of humour
- Outgoing and charming
- Reliable
- Boyish and active
- Intelligent
- Outgoing
- Playful
- Knowledgeable
- Thorough
- Eye for details
- Creative

Cons
- Moody
- Temperamental
- Stressed
- Workaholic
- Self-obsessed
- Pedantic perfectionist
- Split personality
- Emotionally reserved
- Overly health conscious
- Wary of romantic commitment
- Lone wolf
- Critical and analytical
- Worrier
- High expectations

Tip: How to show romantic interest

Appealing to his romantic nature is difficult. Romance is not his strongest side. Making an effort and doing something he doesn't expect you to do will always be interpreted positively.

Hint: Pay attention to his work and interests.

Romantic Vibes

Mr Virgo:
The supportive and inspirational partner

The essence

Reserved. He won't dazzle you with sweet nothings and declare his love for you. He's neither cold nor insensitive; he simply finds it a little difficult to talk about his feelings.

…but makes up for it. When he fails to express something with words, he makes up for it with actions.

Faithful. His partner doesn't have to worry about him running around. He takes commitment seriously.

Loyal. He will always show his woman great respect when out in public.

Romance. A relationship is far more than a romantic affair, it's a source of inspiration. He combines love and friendship and makes his partner his best friend.

Work. His partner must be prepared to compete with his work when days are hectic, but he will never abandon his woman for long – and he will always make it up to her.

Honesty. He is honest and direct in every aspect of his life. If he pays you a compliment, you can be sure he's being sincere.

Inspiring partner. It is very important that his partner is able to inspire him. If she doesn't, he'll get bored.

Tip: How to show erotic interest

Don't be obvious about it. Do and say things which might be interpreted in an erotic manner.

Play with your hair, caress yourself gently while reading or concentrating …anything to make him pay attention – but make it seem casual.

Erotic Vibrations

Mr Virgo:
The cool and analytical lover

The essence

In control. Don't expect a fierce Latin lover to emerge as soon as the clothes are off. This guy is cool in bed as well.

Well prepared. He may ask you about your erotic preferences, simply because he wants everything to be right. Being prepared makes him relax.

Sensual sixth sense. He is a wonderful lover and seems to have a sixth sense when it comes to pleasing his partner.

Conservative - and funky. Although conservative and slightly traditional, he does have a liberal streak…

Erotic hors d'oeuvre. He is a master when it comes to foreplay, but may need a nudge if you don't want to spend hours before getting it on.

All-niter. Stamina is one of his strengths and he can keep going all night.

Open minded - kind of. He is open to suggestions, providing they are not vulgar.

The beauty of sensuality. This man regards sex as an aesthetic experience, not a lesson in breathtaking gymnastics.

CHAPTER 5

COMPATIBILITY QUIZ

Are you banging your head against the wall, or does he unleash your positive potential? Do you provoke him or bring out the best in him? Does he make you throw your arms up in exasperation, or do you feel inspired and complete in his company? Are the two of you headed towards doom or dream? Take the test to find out.

Question 1
What's your attitude to work and ambitions?

A. The sole purpose of a job is to make money.
B. If you want to achieve something in life, you need to make an effort.
C. It depends… I'd probably be more ambitious had my job been more interesting.

Question 2
Do you ever leave things to fate?

A. Never. People who rely on fate are seldom in control of their lives.
B. Sometimes, but only if I have no influence over the outcome of a situation.
C. Of course. Whatever happens, happens.

(cont.)

Question 3.
How do you react when a guy suggests taking a bath or a shower before having sex?

A. That's ok I guess. Never thought much about it.
B. Whenever I'm in a passionate mood, I don't want to run through the shower.
C. I don't mind. Foreplay in the shower can actually be very exciting.

Question 4.
Is it important that your partner clearly expresses his love for you?

A. Yes, I'm no mind reader.
B. My partner and I communicate very well. He only needs to look at me to convey how he feels about me.
C. Yes, but not necessarily with words. There are many other ways to show love and affection.

Question 5.
Would you describe yourself as a physically active person?

A. The only physical activity I'm into is sex.
B. I like hiking and going for walks. I find that very relaxing.
C. I enjoy a wide variety of sports, simply because I enjoy keeping active and staying in shape.

Question 6.
You've decided to seduce you partner one evening. How would you go about it?

A. Give him a sensual bath after a romantic dinner?
B. Depends on his mood, really.
C. Put on sassy underwear and stream a porn movie?

Question 7.
Do you tend to offer constructive criticism and firm advice?

A. Sometimes, but only if I feel it's needed.
B. Very seldom. Friendly hints and diplomacy usually produce better results.
C. Of course. I speak my mind. Honesty is important.

Question 8.
Do you think it's possible to have a rewarding relationship without making sex a major part of your lives?

A. Yes. Sensuality will develop naturally in any loving relationship.
B. No, sex is too important to be pushed aside.
C. I don't know. Erotic impulses make the days more exciting.

Question 9.
How do you feel about guys who suggest having sex on a first date?

A. Well, I'm quite passionate and if the atmosphere turns erotic then why not?
B. I'd be quite offended actually. I think that's cheap.
C. If everything was right. If it was love at first sight. If there's such a thing as dream partner. Until then, I'd probably turn him down.

Question 10.
Do you tend to get easily stressed?

A. Not stressed, but engaged and active. Adrenaline keeps me going.
B. Not really, I'm quite grounded and manage to see things for what they are.
C. Yes, and I tend to worry about things.

SCORE	A	B	C
Question 1	1	10	5
Question 2	10	5	1
Question 3	5	1	10
Question 4	1	10	5
Question 5	1	5	10
Question 6	10	5	1
Question 7	5	10	1
Question 8	10	1	5
Question 9	1	10	5
Question 10	5	10	1

75 – 100

You've finally found the man who brings balance and harmony into your life. You respect his ideals and admire his self-discipline. He makes you feel proud when you're out with friends. You love the way he pampers you and protects you. His unique ability to bring out the best in you, makes you shine. He expects you to be independent and capable of taking care of yourself, but he will always be by your side whenever you need encouragement and a helping hand. A relationship like this will become stronger as time goes by and allow both of you to keep growing. This is a perfect match.

51 – 74

Romantic love and friendship is a perfect combination. This man will give you space as well as treating you to lots of intimacy. He will broaden your horizon with his amazing knowledge - and make you feel like a princess in bed. Life is never boring with Mr. Virgo around. He may get obsessive about detail from time to time, but that's a small price to pay considering all the wonderful things he brings in to your life. He may dish out a few truths from time to time, and give you a verbal kick in the backside if he feels you're getting a tad lazy, but he usually prefers to inspire. When he commits himself to you, you won't have to doubt his love and affection.

26 – 50

This relationship may be a challenge at times, but life is filled with challenges which makes us stronger. Sometimes the two of you seem to be heading off in different directions, which may cause a few discussions. His practical approach may drive you slightly nuts and make you long for a bit more passion in your life. Despite all this, there's something that makes you stay by his side. He is a rare, no-nonsense-guy who makes you feel safe. However, you may reach a point where you need decide. If you keep suppressing your need for excitement and adventure, it will only make you miserable. Life with Mr. Virgo can be hard work, but it can also be very loving and rewarding. In the end it will be a matter of values and what it takes to make both of you happy. Think about it, the choice is yours.

10 – 25

Have you given in to conformity? Have you become a creature of habit, accepting Mr. Virgo's firm suggestions? Are you fascinated by his nice and trim body - which he works out in the gym and not in bed? Are you getting used to playing second fiddle and pushing your own needs and dreams aside? Wake up. Do a reality check and listen to your heart. Be honest with yourself, is there a lot of romance and passion in your life? What are you longing for? Don't waste your life on a partner who's not satisfying your basic needs. He may be nice and kind, but is it worth it? A more suitable partner may be waiting for you elsewhere.

Thoughts...
Love conquers everything, including compatibility guides, partner quizzes and astrological do's and don'ts.

If the man makes you happy, no matter how challenging it might be, give him a chance, give it a try. Just remember, be true to yourself.

LIBRA the male

YOUR DATE: LIBRA
23 September–22 October

The Essence of him

Artistic – creative – kind – diplomatic – restless – charming – genuine – has a strong sense of justice – a lover of beauty – compassionate – fond of people – a romantic drifter – intelligent – indecisive – has a strong work ethic – inclusive – big-hearted – polite – optimistic – attentive – sensual – stands up for people who are not able to do so themselves

...and remember: Aesthetics are important to him, and this applies to every facet of his life. Crudeness, vulgarity and insensitivity provoke him and put him off.

Blind Date – speedy essentials

Who's waiting for you?
Chances are you won't notice him right away – probably because he's already chatting away with another guest or the bartender, and they look like they've known each other for ages. There is something calm and attractive about the Libra man. His attitude and personality appear balanced and relaxed. These guys are seldom big, muscular athletes, but they carry themselves with a gentle masculinity that is very attractive. He will greet you with a warm smile and meet your eyes. Don't worry if you're a bit shy at first. This man will always give you a chance to show your true colours.

Emergency fixes for embarrassing pauses
If you feel the pauses are becoming longer, he could be testing you. Libra men have limited patience for women who have turned off their brains – no matter how beautiful they might be. Take the initiative. Impress him with something he doesn't expect you to know anything about. But make it books – not gossip magazines. Talk exotic music trends – not the latest updates on Twitter.

Your place or mine?
His attitude is calm, collected, polite and charming, but don't be fooled. Behind this distinguished exterior hides a passionate man with a healthy appetite for sex. An overnight on the first date is definitely an option if the two of you hit it off. But if you come on too strong, he might lose interest. For him, no chase means no challenge.

Checklist, before you dash out to meet him:
Tidy yourself up (hair, hands, and eyebrows)
(hint: he'll notice)
Be well rested, with no other engagements
(hint: it might get late)
Be relaxed, with smile in your eyes
(hint: dazzle him)
Wear a feminine and slightly suggestive outfit
(hint: nothing overly sexy)
Brush up on your knowledge of various topics
(hint: inspire him)

Tip: He has a jealous streak. Don't test his interest in you by flirting with other men. It'll have the opposite effect.

CHAPTER 1

PREPARE YOURSELF

Catch his eye, capture his attention
Top 10 attention grabbers

1. Be outgoing, social and cheerful.
2. Be classy. Pay attention to your manners.
3. Show interest in him by asking questions.
4. Avoid eye-popping outfits, even if they are fashionable.
5. Pay attention to your looks, and be carefully groomed from head to toe.
6. Flirt, but be discreet about it. Make him wonder…
7. Emphasise positivity in your views.
8. Show appreciation for people who succeed.
9. Pay him intelligent compliments.
10. Listen and be compassionate.

The SHE. The woman!

As with everything else in his life, his dream woman must inspire him and light up his days with beauty and positivity. He needs more than just a pretty face; inner beauty is very important to him. She must be genuine and interesting, demonstrating joy, positivity, softness and femininity combined with intelligence and independence. These are the characteristics of a real woman – according to him. And it takes a 'real woman' to keep him hooked.

The Essence of her
Feminine – intelligent – attentive – articulate – sensual and passionate – sensible – well-informed and up-to-date about current affairs – interesting, with an independent mind – encouraging and supportive – takes care of herself and her looks – outgoing and friendly in social settings – genuine – compassionate – positive– has an eye for details and the beauty in life

---

Libra arousal meter
From 0 to 100... In 30 minutes. He enjoys taking his time and exploring sensations – and his partner – before getting truly passionate.

Remember: Be true to yourself

It doesn't matter if he is the most stunning guy you've ever met – if you don't match, you don't match. You may be able to put on a show for a while to hold his attention, but what's the point? We can't please everybody. We all have different needs, dreams, tastes and preferences. There's no such thing as a one-size-fits-all lover. Be yourself, and be true to who you are – always!

Very important: If you want to pay him a compliment, make sure it's sincere and slightly out of the ordinary. Pay attention to details.

CHAPTER 2

THE FIRST DATE

Getting your foot in the door
The basics

A catch - and a challenge! It's much easier to capture this guy than to hold onto him. If you want him to hang around for a while – or to establish a more committed relationship – you'll need to start building a solid foundation right away.

Loves women. He may seem fascinated by you, but that doesn't guarantee he'll be there tomorrow. His interest may be genuine, but let's face it: this guy is fascinated by women in general. It takes a special someone to keep him around.

Find the right balance. Take the initiative, but be subtle about it. If you're too assertive, you'll risk pushing him away.

Aesthetics - and inner beauty. Appearance is important. He appreciates the beautiful things in life – and that includes women. You don't have to be a model. What's important is being able to radiate your inner beauty.

Eye contact is crucial. It's actually possible to seduce this guy with only your eyes. This doesn't mean you should stare him down, but playful glances and subtle nonverbal communication will go a long way.

Whatever you do...

- **DON'T** be crude or use rough language.

- **DON'T** gossip or talk negatively about other people.

- **DON'T** come on too strong.

- **DON'T** rely on your looks alone to win him over.

- **DON'T** be aggressive in your views of the world.

Remember,
Never take his interest in you for granted. If you get too comfortable and stop making

- **DON'T** pay him cheap compliments. Be observant about it.

- **DON'T** talk about ex boyfriends or erotic experiences.

- **DON'T** be loud and dominate the conversation.

- **DON'T** be insensitive.

- **DON'T** flirt with other men.

an effort, it may change his perception of you.

Signs you're in - or not

It's not easy to tell with a Libra man, because he doesn't want to hurt your feelings. He could be polite, friendly and forthcoming ... but after that, he's just as likely to fade out as he is to call you. Is he staying or going? You'll have to give it a few days. It won't hurt to be assertive through a text message, but do it seductively and in a feminine way. Make sure you don't come across as aggressive. Yes, he may need a gentle nudge at times, but be careful not to nudge him out of your life. There will be obvious signs that you've captured his interest:

Chances are he will...

- return your calls immediately
- invite you out or to his home – just the two of you!
- be very attentive to your needs in bed
- ask for your opinion about things that are important to him
- include you in his plans
- act romantic and amorous

Not your type? Making an exit

Chances are that Mr. Libra will have taken off long before you start thinking about ways to call it off. He is a drifter, a dreamer and in a constant search for beauty. Combine this with a healthy appetite for the hunt, and you have someone who won't stick around for long if things aren't working out. He sees life as too precious to be wasted on a fling that's leading nowhere. And he has a big circle of friends who are

are more than happy to introduce new opportunities into his life.

However, there is always an exception to the rule: this is the Libra guy who stays around, hoping it might work out and thinking that you're just having a bad day or a bad week … or a bad month. It's rare, but if you have dazzled him, it could happen. Don't let guilt stand in the way of happiness – for both of you. Put your foot down.

Foolproof exit measures:

If these measures don't work, you've probably got his star sign wrong. They may seem a little over the top, but for a Libra, they're sure to do the trick.

- Act like a drama queen with daily mood swings
- Tell him to speed up while having sex
- Ask him why spends so much time thinking: how about some action?
- Introduce him to some of your loud, athletic male friends (even if you have to borrow some vague acquaintances for the occasion)
- Tell him you are reinventing yourself and start wearing tacky clothes
- End every sentence with 'duh' or 'whatever'

CHAPTER 3

SEX'N STUFF

Seductive moves:
How to get him in the mood:

The Libra is one of the most aesthetic guys in the zodiac. His life is ruled by beauty and harmony – and this extends to any erotic encounter. He will respond positively to setting the mood: candles, soft pillows, a faint exotic scent, a glass of Champagne... you get the idea. He is attracted to women who manage to be passionate without appearing vulgar, and he values softness and femininity.

Preferences and erotic nature

He may sometimes need a firm and guiding partner to get him started, but as soon as his erotic feelings are lit, he will do virtually anything to please you. The only thing he won't do is rush things. He enjoys taking his time, fully exploring his partner's body and his own sensations, and giving and receiving gentle touches. This may not sound particularly passionate to you, but his soft sensuality can drive any woman wild with desire. Besides, he's no innocent little boy, and he may be open to frisky suggestions – provided they are not too crude or vulgar.

Hitting the right buttons

Although every sign has areas that are more sensitive than others, individual sensitivity may vary quite a bit. Don't go body-blind. Honing in on these erogenous zones and forgetting the rest of him is not a good idea. Use his erogenous zones to create sparks while turning him on, and as a passion booster when it gets heated. Watch his body language – including the most obvious of signs! Open your mind to the sensuality of touch and taste.

Key areas
Lower back and the buttocks

Get it on
The lower back and his buttocks are the key areas for this guy – and they're conveniently located, as they give you ample opportunity to stimulate him in public as well. Walking with your arms around each other's waists will provide an easy way to get him going - and make him want to pick up the pace in order to get back home as quickly as possible.

Arouse him
Start off by giving him an innocent massage. He loves having his bum massaged, both lightly and more deeply. If you really want him to groan with passion, you can start biting, licking and sucking his bum while gently scratching his lower back with your fingernails. Be prepared for some wild desire...

Surprise him

He gets a kick out of doing innocent things he's not supposed to do, like looking at you while you're getting undressed. Make this easy for him: leave the door slightly ajar and sensually apply lotion to your naked body – pretending you don't know he's secretly watching you.

Spice it up

Watching and being watched is a big turn-on for this guy. Suggest taking turns pleasing each other. Don't rush it. Take your time and make it sensual.

Remember: Although he may take a little while to get started, this man can go all night. Guide him gently.

His expectations

Blissful pleasure. No need to worry if you don't feel super energetic. Sometimes, it's pure bliss to lie back and enjoy being stimulated. Mr Libra doesn't mind spoiling you with sensual pleasures – provided you don't start getting lazy in bed.

Soft and sassy. His ideal partner will be feminine in bed, but he doesn't mind a little creativity.

Be original. He welcomes original ideas and suggestions, as long as they're not crude or vulgar.

Take your time. He expects his partner to appreciate the sensual and gentle nuances of sex and not to rush things. Taking time to explore and enjoy is very important to him. Orgasm chasers won't be invited back in to his bed. He loves lengthy foreplay and slowly building intense passion and pleasure.

Be present, embrace the moment. Slow caresses and gentle touches are essential for intimacy with this man.

Your sensual preferences
Quiz yourself and find out whether this man is for you.

Where on the scale are you?
1 = Don't agree | 3 = Sure | 5 = Agree!

1. Touch, taste and smell is very important during sex.
One a scale for 1 to 5, you are: 1 - 2 - 3- 4 - 5

2. Taking it slow is the best way to fully experience erotic pleasure.
One a scale for 1 to 5, you are: 1 - 2 - 3- 4 - 5

3. Watching each other experience pleasure can be arousing and satisfying.
One a scale for 1 to 5, you are: 1 - 2 - 3- 4 - 5

4. Vulgar language and smutty sex toys etc, can ruin the sensual pleasures of sex.
One a scale for 1 to 5, you are: 1 - 2 - 3- 4 - 5

Score 15–20: Excellent! With this kind of harmony, your erotic interactions will be intense and fulfilling.
Score 10–14: You may be able to strike the perfect balance between giving and taking. Feel free to be creative and take the initiative.
Score 5–9: Resist the urge to rush. Enjoy the slower sensual pleasures, and you may discover new erotic horizons.
Score 1–4: Allow yourself to experience sex using all your senses. This will help you enjoy every moment, not just the climax.

CHAPTER 4

GENERAL STUFF

The big picture

Keep in mind that the characteristics of a Libra may vary quite a bit depending on where within the sign he was born, as well as a wide range of additional astrological factors. But for now, let's stick to the basics. Just remember: don't jump to conclusions as soon as you meet him. Give him room to shine. Get to know the man behind the sign.

His personality: Pros and cons

Pros
- Compassionate
- Intelligent
- Romantic
- Sensitive
- Sensual
- Polite and gallant
- Generous
- Intuitive
- Diplomatic
- Enthusiastic
- Social
- An excellent host
- Has a strong work ethic
- Has a strong sense of justice

Cons
- Indecisive
- Restless
- Temperamental
- Commitment-avoidant
- Possessive
- Jealous
- Evasive
- Falls easily in and out of love
- Insensitive when busy
- Builds castles in the sky
- Emotionally detached
- Avoidant of personal conflicts
- Impractical
- Moody

Tip: How to show romantic interest

Interestingly enough, the initiative for romance usually comes from Mr. Libra. He is not particularly shy, and if you have managed to spark his interest, he won't waste any time before taking it further. At this point, all you have to do is play along.

Romantic Vibes

Mr Libra:
The dreamy and restless partner

The essence

Never take anything for granted. The Libra man loves women, and it's a lot easier to catch him than to hold onto him. Be on your toes and make an effort.

Embraces beauty. He's not really a womanizer – he just appreciates beauty and the sensuous side of life. Combine this with his indecision, and you get a guy whose interest will only be captured by someone very special.

A dreamer. He is always searching for the perfect love. This is what causes him to avoid casually entering into committed relationships.

The complete package. A stunning beauty will always be a great hit, but only for so long. Although he may feel proud to be seen with her, he won't be bothered with someone who cannot inspire him.

Clever and inspiring. A feminine and creative woman who makes him think stands the best chance of holding onto him. This may seem like hard work at times, but Mr Libra is worth it.

The big prize: He is a romantic, attentive and sensitive partner who will do his utmost to make life wonderful for his woman.

Tip: How to show erotic interest

This man is a master when it comes to observing people. He picks up on moods very quickly. Take advantage of this by focusing on sensual feelings, and communicating with your eyes. As soon as he becomes curious, add some suggestive body language.

Erotic Vibrations

Mr Libra:
The gentle and attentive lover

The essence

Passion and determination. Although he may come across as a polite gentleman, this is a very passionate guy who wants to make his partner happy - even if it takes all night.

The chase. Sex is important to a Libra – and so is the chase. Sometimes, the chase becomes the most important element, and he may lose interest if the woman doesn't live up to his expectations once he's caught her.

Sensual sixth sense. He is a determined lover who seems to know exactly what you want and when. Sometimes he may come across as a mind reader.

No need to fake it. Don't suggest anything kinky, which is not really your thing, simply because you think *he may* like it. He'll probably just smile at you and start pleasing *you* in the way he knows you want to be pleased.

Take it easy. He needs to move at his own pace. Remember not to push him.

A firm nudge! His indecisive personality may mean that you sometimes have to make decisions for him – like whether and when to make love, the bedroom or the bathroom, and so on. But these are details. Overall, this guy is an erotic dream.

CHAPTER 5

COMPATIBILITY QUIZ

Are you banging your head against the wall, or does he unleash your positive potential? Do you provoke him or bring out the best in him? Does he make you throw your arms up in exasperation, or do you feel inspired and complete in his company? Are the two of you headed towards doom or dream? Take the test to find out.

Question 1.
How do you feel about long, sensual foreplay?

A. Love it. It's a wonderful way to build up to climax.
B. Not my thing. Drawn-out foreplay tends to make me restless and impatient.
C. It's nice, provided it doesn't ruin the passion and creativity!

Question 2.
Once upon a time, there was a lonely prince... How would you continue this story?

A. There are no princes, only frogs!
B. ...who finally found his princess, and they lived happily ever after.
C. ...who turned out to be just a charming Casanova.

(cont.)

Question 3.
Do you expect your partner to express his thoughts and feelings clearly?

A. Well, he doesn't have to spell it out, provided we both understand each other.
B. Not really. His feelings can be conveyed through expressions and body language.
C. Yes. An introverted enigma is not my type.

Question 4.
A guy you've just met shows up at your door with a bunch of flowers. How do you react?

A. I'd be surprised, obviously – but also happy and flattered.
B. There are creepy nutters everywhere. I'd slam the door in his face.
C. If only! How come that only happens in commercials? I'd love a guy like that!

Question 5.
How would you describe your ideal guy?

A. Sporty and athletic.
B. Interesting and romantic.
C. Rich, generous and handsome.

Question 6.
If the setting was right, which of the following would be your preferred place to make love?

A. On a secluded beach in the moonlight.
B. In a comfortable and romantic setting, most likely at home.
C. Under the covers with the lights off.

Question 7.
Do you tend to postpone things?

A. I must admit that I do – especially chores and boring tasks.
B. Yes! I'm always late with everything.
C. No, not really. I'm pretty structured.

Question 8.
You're set on seducing a guy. What's your trick?

A. Emphasizing my feminine side.
B. I don't like seducing men.
C. Putting on a sassy outfit.

Question 9.
Do you like to keep yourself up-to-date with what's going on in the world?

A. Absolutely. I know everything there is to know about celebrities.
B. I'm about average, I guess. I watch the news and read newspapers most days.
C. Yes, I enjoy keeping myself informed. I love in depth stories

Question 10.
Would you describe yourself as emotional?

A. I'm romantic and sensitive, but not really emotional.
B. Yes, I can be, especially if someone hurts my feelings.
C. No. I don't get emotional. If I'm upset I put my foot down right away.

SCORE	A	B	C
Question 1	10	1	5
Question 2	1	10	5
Question 3	5	10	1
Question 4	5	1	10
Question 5	1	10	5
Question 6	10	5	1
Question 7	1	5	10
Question 8	10	1	5
Question 9	1	5	10
Question 10	10	1	5

75 – 100
Whatever you guys are doing, keep on doing it – it works! You don't even have to think about it; harmony just happens. You're finely tuned to each other's needs, and it's easy to make adventures happen. You share the same values when it comes to freedom, beauty, justice and sensuality. You are open-minded and flexible, and you would never betray each other's trust. This is a great match. Enjoy life – and each other.

51 – 74
Finally, you have met a man who has the ability to make you feel happy and loved, broaden your horizons, expand your vision and dreams and enlighten your spiritual self … so don't mess up! Sure, his mind does seem to drift off every now and then, but this might even appeal to you. He is always searching, appreciating what's around him – and living. People pay thousands to attend seminars to make them mindful and in tune with the moment. This guy doesn't need that. His life is made up of individual moments – and maybe this is why he makes you feel so alive. Right now, you're here, enjoying the moment. The two of you have found something special. If you make an effort, it will continue to grow.

26 – 50

Well … he may be a treasure, or he may be a pain. This depends on your values, your expectations and your attitude. You probably wish there was a bit more action and a little less talk. A bit more strength and masculinity; a little less poetry by candlelight. His sensitivity attracts you, but you long for a man who has his feet on the ground. Maybe you fell for this guy because of his interest in you – but that interest will shift easily to someone else unless you can manage to hold onto it. Love should flow freely. This one is up to you, really: you could make an effort and see how it goes, or you could look for someone who makes you feel love more effortlessly.

10 – 25

Let's be blunt about this. A once-off encounter could be fun. Anything beyond that will be a challenge – a big challenge. You have completely different outlooks on life. Your expectations are different. Your attitudes towards masculinity are different. But you won't have to worry about making a decision for the two of you. If things are not running smoothly, Mr Libra will move on without any trace of drama. Your ideal partner – and true happiness – is waiting somewhere else.

Thoughts...
Are you taking on a challenge for the right reasons? Are you seeing him, or are you seeing that man you wish he were? Happiness is precious. Embrace it - either with or without him. However, never leave without giving love a chance.

SCORPIO the male

YOUR DATE: SCORPIO
23 October–21 November

The Essence of him

Mysterious – sensual – intense – direct – reserved – charming – entertaining – interesting and knowledgeable – strongly influenced by his surroundings – cultivated and philosophical – suspicious – a good judge of character – needs control – kind – considerate – protective and loyal – sensitive – vindictive – supportive – has a good memory – creative – jealous

…and remember: Although this man is direct and to the point, he will wait until he knows you really well to open up about his feelings and who he is, deep down.

Blind Date – speedy essentials

Who's waiting for you?
It's the guy who looks at you as you enter the room. Yes, he will be smiling, but that's not what gets you. The intensity of his gaze … it's impossible to ignore. It will either make you a little nervous or very attracted, or both. All of this will happen quickly, even before he's had a chance to say hi. There's something magnetic and mysterious about him, something you can't put your finger on. This is what makes him so fascinating. He's an enigma, waiting to be explored and discovered. But be yourself. This man is a good judge of character and will notice if you try to fool him.

Emergency fixes for embarrassing pauses
Chances are slim that a Scorpio man will ever run out of things to talk about – but that doesn't mean there won't be a pause or two. This man communicates with his eyes. What you may interpret as an embarrassing pause may actually be a flirtation or a suggestion – or an erotic invitation. If you can handle this, you can handle a date with Mr Scorpio.

Your place or mine?
Love is not an important ingredient in this man's sex life. He's very passionate, and if he likes you, it won't be long before the casual conversation moves to the next level. The foreplay can actually start before you leave the restaurant. Weird? Not with this guy. He is a master of seduction. If you allow yourself to sink into his eyes, you may discover this yourself…

Checklist, before you dash out to meet him:
No heavy eye makeup
(hint: communicate with your yes)
Put your phone on silent
(hint: no guys calling you!)
Wear seductive underwear
(hint: you will radiate sensuality)
Wear a sassy and feminine outfit
(hint: nothing tacky)
Smile and make your voice lively
(hint: make him laugh and feel happy)

Tip: *Never* give the impression that you're interested in something without seeing it through, especially not when it comes to sex. You don't play around with this guy. A yes is a yes!

CHAPTER 1

PREPARE YOURSELF

Catch his eye, capture his attention
Top 10 attention grabbers

1. Be sparkling; make him laugh.
2. Be direct without being blunt.
3. Show attentiveness and affection.
4. Play along with his ideas and offer constructive opinions.
5. Wear something that will emphasise your curves.
6. Suggest new and interesting places to go: a small restaurant, an intimate club, etc.
7. Don't make yourself too accessible. He loves a challenge.
8. Make sure you have something interesting to tell him. Pay attention to details.
9. Use your eyes to communicate, and be sensual about it.
10. Be outgoing and social.

The SHE. The woman!

The Scorpio man wants a little bit of everything. It can be difficult to figure out which qualities make the 'must have' list. He is a passionate guy, and he seeks the same passion in his woman. She must be attractive and sexy. It's also important that she's intelligent, loyal and supportive. But without chemistry, communication will be difficult. If there's no chemistry, there's no future.

The Essence of her
Cheerful – erotic – flexible – sharp, with an independent mind – has a positive attitude and a constructive outlook – loyal – supportive – genuine – sexy, both in mind and appearance – liberated – faithful – passionate in bed – sensual and erotically playful – optimistic – feminine – assertive without being aggressive – attentive and admiring

Scorpio arousal meter
From 0 to 100... In an instant! A calm and laid-back Scorpio can transform himself into a passionate dream very quickly. Be prepared.

Remember: Be true to yourself

It doesn't matter if he is the most stunning guy you've ever met – if you don't match, you don't match. You may be able to put on a show for a while to hold his attention, but what's the point? We can't please everybody. We all have different needs, dreams, tastes and preferences. There's no such thing as a one-size-fits-all lover. Be yourself, and be true to who you are – always!

Very important: He can read your mood, body language and expressions. Don't try to hide anything from him. Got something on your mind? Let it out.

CHAPTER 2

THE FIRST DATE

Getting your foot in the door
The basics

A touch of mystery. He loves a challenge, so don't make yourself too accessible. This doesn't mean you should play hard to get, but resist throwing yourself at him. Show interest, but keep a slight distance.

Joy! He loves women who can make him laugh and bring out the bright side of life, so make sure to show him your sparkling and playful side.

Easy on the jokes. Take him seriously. Making jokes on his behalf, no matter how innocently, is a no-no! It will turn him off you completely.

He'll call your bluff. He observes, analyses and interprets body language with great ease. If you put on a show, he will call your bluff. Never try to impress him by being someone you're not – anyway, why would you?

Be flexible - and genuine! Keep an open mind. Be flexible. Stubborn discussions give him a headache. Be genuine. If you pay him a compliment, make sure you mean it.

Whatever you do...

- **DON'T** flirt with other men (!).

- **DON'T** signal that you're erotically interested if you're not.

- **DON'T** dismiss his ideas. Take him seriously.

- **DON'T** provoke him or start an argument unnecessarily.

- **DON'T** be too critical

Remember, he can spot a fake quickly. Be open. Be genuine. Be yourself.

- **DON'T** be shy. Return his direct glance.

- **DON'T** be negative in your views of the world.

- **DON'T** dress too conservatively.

- **DON'T** ignore him and start talking to others.

- **DON'T** betray his trust.

He is very supportive, provided you play it straight.

Signs you're in - or not

The Scorpio is a passionate man, and he's either in or he's out. If he likes you, he will let you know – but in his own way. When it comes to showing feelings and romantic interest, he prefers nonverbal communication or actions. Words tend to get a little awkward for him. If you are on the same level and able to read each other by observing, this won't be a problem. However, if you're not familiar with his style of communicating, the following signs may indicate that he's got his eyes on you:

Chances are he will...

- call you the same evening
- be supportive of your ideas
- organise something for you to do together, maybe a trip
- treat you to coffee or dinners
- be focused on you and won't notice other women in the room
- be eager to be physically close to you

Not your type? Making an exit

Don't worry – a relationship with a Scorpio will seldom come to the point of needing to stage an escape. Although he bonds quickly with someone who sparks his romantic interest, he disappears just as abruptly if things aren't working out. Sure, he may slam a few doors, wave his arms around and raise his voice, but that's about it – and then he'll be gone. Minimally, he needs a woman who he can relate to, who's supportive and who can make his days pleasant and passionate. Why would he waste time on someone who can't provide the basics?

However, some unusual Scorpio men may become stuck in a fantasy. They fail to grasp reality and reach for a dream that faded ages ago. In this case, you don't have much choice but to be blunt about it. Prepare yourself. There will be passionate arguments – but he will eventually realise that a more rewarding relationship awaits him elsewhere.

Foolproof exit measures:

These tips are far from nice. However, if you really want to send him a message, any of the following will do the trick.

- Tell him you're not in the mood for sex and that he can go ahead and please himself without you
- When you do have sex, complain about his lovemaking and insist on doing things your way
- Flirt with other men whenever you're out together
- Pursue your own interests alone in the evenings
- Joke around whenever he wants to have a serious conversation
- Be stubborn and inflexible. Turn every little gripe into a major discussion

CHAPTER 3

SEX'N STUFF

Seductive moves:
How to get him in the mood:

He is an adventurous guy who is open to suggestions. Teasing can make him go wild, but don't confuse this with playing hard to get. Pretending not to be interested – if you are – is a turn-off. If she does things right, a woman who is playful and sensual can bring out his passion. Stripping is a great example of this, especially if you don't allow him to touch you.

Preferences and erotic nature

A Scorpio man wants to dazzle you, surprise you, please you and dominate you, all at the same time – and he usually succeeds. He knows exactly what to do and will probably discover erogenous zones you never knew you had. Soft cuddles and sweet kisses won't do it for him. He feeds on passion and intensity, and he wants you to come on strong – but without being aggressive. He doesn't mind using sexual gadgets in order to explore sensations and satisfy his partner and himself. But don't make the mistake of thinking he doesn't know what to do with his hands. He's an expert!

Hitting the right buttons

Although every sign has areas that are more sensitive than others, individual sensitivity may vary quite a bit. Don't go body-blind. Honing in on these erogenous zones and forgetting the rest of him is not a good idea. Use his erogenous zones to create sparks while turning him on, and as a passion booster when it gets heated. Watch his body language – including the most obvious of signs! Open your mind to the sensuality of touch and taste.

Key areas
His genitals

Get it on
All things erotic combine in this man: he loves women, he loves the chase – provided it doesn't go on for ever – and he loves sex. And his erogenous zone? His genitals! No matter how complicated he may seem, pleasing him is simple and straightforward.

Arouse him
Star signs with less obvious erogenous zones are easier to arouse in public – it can be as simple as touching their hands, back or legs. Not so with Mr Scorpio. Casually stimulating his genitals in a public place requires creativity. Crowded rooms and tightly packed queues could provide a chance to get close to him. You could always ask to feel the fabric of his trousers… But remember, as soon as he's aroused, he will not be easily contained. Don't fool around with this guy!

Surprise him
A big turn-on for this man is a woman who can undress him with her eyes in a public place. If the sexual chemistry between you is strong, it won't take long before he starts getting hot … start practising!

Spice it up
Scorpio is a water sign, which means he loves showering with you – and rubbing his body against yours while you're at it. Oils and creams usually produce positive results. Be creative.

Remember: Never start something you don't intend to finish. As soon as you have turned him on, there will be no looking back.

His expectations

Lots of tenderness. His ideal partner is warm, tender and passionate.

Running the show. He's not too keen on sexually aggressive women. Playing second fiddle is not his style. However, a passive partner is even worse – he finds it boring.

Don't be shy, be loud. His partner must show interest, take the initiative and clearly display how she feels – preferably in a physical way.

Erotic enigmas. He loves when his partner provides with the erotic inspiration that allows him to explore the mysteries of sex even further.

Feeling free. Sexual chemistry is very important to him. His partner needs to be on the same level in order for him to feel truly liberated and uninhibited.

There is a time and place... Careful playfulness can be a great kick, provided it happens before things get too hot and steamy.

Embrace passion. The most important things of all is that his partner must clearly show appreciation for his intense passion.

Your sensual preferences
Quiz yourself and find out whether this man is for you.

Where on the scale are you?
1 = Don't agree | 3 = Sure | 5 = Agree!

1. Sex without intense passion and intensity is not worth having.
One a scale for 1 to 5, you are: 1 - 2 - 3- 4 - 5

2. Too much sensitivity and gentle kissing can ruin the passion.
One a scale for 1 to 5, you are: 1 - 2 - 3- 4 - 5

3. A strong and dominating partner makes it easier to display passion in bed.
One a scale for 1 to 5, you are: 1 - 2 - 3- 4 - 5

4. New positions and gadgets are important for keeping a sex life satisfying.
One a scale for 1 to 5, you are: 1 - 2 - 3- 4 - 5

Score 15–20: Fierce – intense – passionate – satisfying – 100% wow.

10 - 14: This man can bring you to new heights and make you feel amazing. Sometimes, you may need to make an effort to keep up with him.

5 - 9: He'll sweep you off your feet in no time, but things may become a little too intense in the long run. Talk to him. He wants to please you, so he will adjust.

1 - 4: Be prepared: this is a passionate guy. He could open new erotic doors for you – or, if you're not into it, shut down the erotic vibes completely.

CHAPTER 4

GENERAL STUFF

The big picture

Keep in mind that the characteristics of a Scorpio may vary quite a bit depending on where within the sign he was born, as well as a wide range of additional astrological factors. But for now, let's stick to the basics. Just remember: don't jump to conclusions as soon as you meet him. Give him room to shine. Get to know the man behind the sign.

His personality: Pros and cons

Pros
- Mysterious and sensual
- Intense and direct
- Persistent
- Creative
- Energetic
- Passionate
- Sensitive
- An excellent observer
- Knowledgeable
- A good judge of character
- Kind and considerate
- Protective and loyal
- Courageous
- Thorough

Cons
- Jealous
- Stubborn
- Domineering
- Temperamental
- Reserved
- Suspicious
- Controlling
- Evasive
- Vindictive
- Secretive
- Ruthless
- Arrogant
- Possessive
- Unforgiving

Tip: How to show romantic interest

Be direct. Show interest in him – not only as a man, but as a person with an interesting life. Be supportive and affectionate. Let him know he can trust you.

Romantic Vibes

Mr Scorpio:
The protective and loyal partner

The essence

Love is everything. When this man falls in love, he falls deeply. Superficial flings and casual romantic affairs do not exist in his world. Love absorbs him, and he feels it intensely.

…and love is never a chore! Although he bonds easily with a woman who has captured his heart, she should never take him, nor his feelings, for granted. This man does not waste his time.

Sparks might fly. Love and chemistry are the essence of his relationships, which require constant nourishment in order to grow.

A bumpy ride. He is no easy partner – in fact, he can be quite the challenge. Although he's kind and generous, he can also be jealous, temperamental and demanding.

Pick up the signals. Women who need vocal and direct affirmation will probably find his nonverbal approach a bit frustrating. His partner must be able to interpret his tone of voice, the way he looks at her and his body language.

Get close. He truly enjoys intimacy and privacy. A super-social Scorpio may turn into a homebody when he finds the woman of his dreams.

Tip: How to show erotic interest

If you know how to communicate with him, showing erotic interest is easy. Allow your glance to linger on him, give him playful smiles and touch him gently with the tips of your fingers.

Erotic Vibrations

Mr Scorpio:
The intense and passionate lover

The essence

Keep the fire alive. If you long for regular, passionate, sexual encounters, this guy comes close to being the ultimate erotic dream.

Getting on top of things. Sometimes, he may come across as slightly dominating in bed. Don't be put off by this – it's just one of many ways that he gets his kicks.

Extensive menu. He can get into virtually anything, provided it gives you pleasure! In his attempts to please you, he may get slightly carried away at times. If this happens, just tell him to slow down a bit.

Take part, be active. Don't be fooled into thinking you can just lay back and enjoy the whole thing! A Scorpio man will expect you to play an active role. If you fail to do so, he will probably start wondering what's wrong, and he'll eventually lose interest.

Endurance. His energy seems to last for ever. This guy can go all night without tiring!

Imagination rules. Just when you think that the two of you have tried everything under the sun, Mr Scorpio will suggest something new and exciting.

CHAPTER 5

COMPATIBILITY QUIZ

Are you banging your head against the wall, or does he unleash your positive potential? Do you provoke him or bring out the best in him? Does he make you throw your arms up in exasperation, or do you feel inspired and complete in his company? Are the two of you headed towards doom or dream? Take the test to find out.

Question 1.
How do you deal with a jealous partner?

A. It annoys me. I wish my man would trust me more.
B. Even though it makes me roll my eyes, I actually find it flattering and reassuring. It's a way to know he cares.
C. I would never give him reason to be. Why would I flirt with other men when I have the world's greatest partner?

Question 2.
You're out having dinner with a guy you've just met. How do you respond when he starts gazing deeply into your eyes?

A. I'd probably get nervous and start playing with my napkin...
B. I'd ask him if he lost a contact lens.
C. I'd return his gaze with a sensual one of my own, and we'd take it from there...

(cont.)

Question 3.
Do you think it's possible to communicate without words?

A. How else are you supposed to communicate?!
B. Yes, absolutely. Sometimes, a glance can say more than a thousand words.
C. It depends on the situation. Words are occasionally necessary to avoid misunderstandings.

Question 4.
Do you enjoy flirting for its own sake?

A. No. I only flirt when I want to accomplish something.
B. Sometimes, but I never intend to hurt anybody.
C. Of course. It's game; everybody knows that. I enjoy sparking interest in men.

Question 5.
Do you tend to dish out comments and opinions without thinking?

A. Very seldom. I don't like getting hurt, so I'm careful to risk hurting others.
B. If criticism is called for, I'm blunt and direct about it. People need to be able to handle the truth.
C. Sometimes, but only if I'm angry.

Question 6.
What's your attitude to sex?

A. Sex? Sweaty and boring. I'm not into it, actually.
B. Although I enjoy sex, whether or not I'm up for it depends on my mood.
C. Sex and passion are essential in a relationship. Without them, it's just a friendship.

Question 7.
Do you need many people around you to thrive?

A. Not really – especially if I'm in a loving and passionate relationship.
B. It's not important, provided my partner and I get out and socialise from time to time.
C. I have an active social life and thrive with people around me. Spending time on my own makes me feel restless.

Question 8.
Are you stubborn in discussions with your partner?

A. Rarely. Flexibility usually produces more positive results.
B. Yes. My partner is stubborn, and it provokes me.
C. Sometimes, but only if the topic is really important to me.

Question 9.
Would you describe yourself as optimistic?

A. Most of the time, but I never lose sight of reality.
B. Yes. Being positive is a game-changer. You can achieve so much more.
C. Above all, I'm realistic. Then I can add optimism and enthusiasm, if it's appropriate.

Question 10.
What are your preferences in bed?

A. Soft, sensitive and romantic.
B. Creative, erotic and tender.
C. Hot, passionate and intense.

SCORE	A	B	C
Question 1	1	5	10
Question 2	5	1	10
Question 3	1	10	5
Question 4	10	5	1
Question 5	10	1	5
Question 6	1	5	10
Question 7	5	10	1
Question 8	10	1	5
Question 9	5	10	1
Question 10	1	5	10

75 – 100
Suddenly, there he was, pushing all of the competition aside. He dazzled you and swept you off your feet. You're probably still amazed by it. Life is never boring with him. He brings out the passion in you and makes you experience life in a completely different way; he makes you feel alive. It's almost as if he has kissed you out of a deep sleep, like in a fairy tale – a very passionate fairy tale. In return, you provide him with the love, support and reassurance he needs to feel safe and grounded. It's a good match. Enjoy each other!

51 – 74
The two of you have a unique way of communicating – it sometimes feels as if you can read each other's minds. But that doesn't mean you always agree. There might be a rumble of thunder from time to time, but a thunderstorm always leaves the air clear and refreshing. You are well aware that behind the macho exterior hides a sensitive boy, and you would never do anything to hurt him. In fact, you feel very protective towards him. He admires your calmness, patience and your ability to bring out the sunshine, no matter how grey the day. You also bring out the passion in him – and that's something you can both fully enjoy. There's excellent harmony here, and wonderful days ahead...

26 – 50

You're either extremely patient and flexible – or you are head over heels in love. The way things are now, you probably find yourself sacrificing to make things work. But how long are you prepared to do so? There are limits to everything. If you give too much and get little fulfillment in return, the warm feelings will eventually fade. You have two options: you can either tell him about your frustrations and give him a chance to adjust – or you can recognise that the man of your dreams is waiting somewhere else. But don't wait too long. Nothing will happen until you take the first step. The only question is whether to step into the relationship or out of it...

10 – 25

He is a mystery, an erotic challenge – and someone who provokes you endlessly. Is it curiosity that makes you stay, or are you doing it out of habit? Or, perhaps, are you waiting to teach him a lesson? This won't be productive. Staying for the wrong reasons will yield the wrong results. Isn't it time you committed to finding true love – and a sex life that brings you pleasure? You need someone different in your life, and he probably does too. Let it go. Move on with your life. Love, sensuality and happiness await you both elsewhere.

Thoughts...
Things may not always be as they seem. Don't rely on a quiz to give you big answers - talk to him and embrace the positive feelings.

SAGITTARIUS the male

YOUR DATE: SAGITTARIUS
22 November–21 December

The Essence of him

Charming – positive – enthusiastic – frank – outspoken – honest – empathetic – capable of viewing a topic from many angles – restless – attentive – energetic – often ahead of his time – intelligent – kind – disorganized – boyish – adventurous – idealistic – entertaining – in love with love – impulsive – values freedom

...and remember: Although he seems genuinely interested in you, you'll have to make an effort to hold on to him. He won't settle for a pretty face – he needs a stimulating mind as well.

Blind Date – speedy essentials

Who's waiting for you?
Don't get upset if he doesn't notice you right away. This is a social guy and he's probably talking to the people at the neighbouring table, the waitress or the bartender. He can actually get so carried away that he forgets why he's there in the first place – until you show up, of course. He's an expert when it comes to living for the moment, which makes him easily distracted. This is no fashion-conscious man wearing the latest trends and sporting a sharp haircut. His style is comfortable, relaxed, stylish and classy. However, what really makes you notice him is his attitude: he's alive and engaged.

Emergency fixes for embarrassing pauses
Don't worry! This man will have taken off long before embarrassing pauses become an issue. If he senses that the two of you have very little in common, he will probably make an excuse – or even tell you directly – and take off. However, if you should come across a shy Sagittarius (which is very rare), your best bet is to talk about exotic places you have visited or fun and exciting experiences. Steer clear of anything negative: you want to create a positive atmosphere, not a cloud of doom.

Your place or mine?
Some people might claim that he refuses to grow up, which really isn't true. He grows up but keeps the boy inside – which is reflected in so many areas in his life, as well as his sex life. Sex is fun and exciting, so why not embrace the opportunity when it arises? Although he'd never say so, he firmly believes himself to be a great lover. Whether this is true or not depends very much on his partner's preferences.

Checklist, before you dash out to meet him:
- Wear heels
(hint: He loves women's legs)
- Use a nice, light scent – nothing heavy
(hint: Make him sense you)
- No deep cleavage
(hint: Leave something to his imagination)
- Leave your worries at home
(hint: Keep it positive)
- Bring your appetite
(hint: For food, knowledge and fun

Tip: Greet him with joy and enthusiasm. Be positive around him. If you don't agree with him, offer constructive views and intelligent questions.

CHAPTER 1

PREPARE YOURSELF

Catch his eye, capture his attention
Top 10 attention grabbers

1. A positive and sparkling personality.
2. A feminine outfit which leaves a lot to his imagination.
3. Good legs, preferably with high heels (but classy, not cheap).
4. Unusual ideas and interesting comments.
5. Playfulness and being a slight tease.
6. Not being afraid to stand out in a crowd, in a positive way.
7. Sending hints, without being obvious about the intention.
8. Asking interesting questions.
9. Coming up with spontaneous suggestions.
10. Being adventurous and loving trying new things.

The SHE. The woman!

A good-looking woman can make him look twice, but it takes more to capture his interest. He must feel he's on the same wavelength as her – otherwise there's no point. She must be "real" and convey a natural beauty. She must be eloquent, sparkling and positive with a sharp mind. He doesn't mind if she sticks out in the crowd – this only makes her exciting! Shy and timid women are not his obvious choice, but neither are aggressive ones. The woman of his dreams must be able to handle his ironic sense of humour, be outgoing, independent, feminine, optimistic, spontaneous and adventurous. In other words, she must be his playmate in the playground of life.

The Essence of her
Feminine but strong – impulsive – attentive to his needs – positive outlook on life – creative – supportive of his ideas – independent, but still a solid rock in his life – has an independent mind – not afraid of standing on her own feet – takes care of herself and her body – has sunshine in her eyes – sensual and playful – a good sense of humour – doesn't take herself too seriously – adventurous – loves to travel.

Sagittarius arousal meter
From 0 to 100... In 10 minutes. If you manage to hit the right buttons, he'll be ready for you in no time. In other words, never start anything you don't intend to finish!

Remember: Be true to yourself
It doesn't matter if he is the most stunning guy you've ever met – if you don't match, you don't match. You may be able to put on a show for a while to hold his attention, but what's the point? We can't please everybody. We all have different needs, dreams, tastes and preferences. There's no such thing as a one-size-fits-all lover. Be yourself, and be true to who you are – always!

Very important: Be positive. The Sagittarius male really dislikes pessimistic and negative people. Avoid gossip, bad news and negative stories.

CHAPTER 2

THE FIRST DATE

Getting your foot in the door
The basics

Ease into it. Take the initiative, but be careful. This guy gets all nervous if he suspects someone is trying to tie him down.

Be classy. He appreciates style and good taste, while bad language can turn him off you completely.

...and interesting. When you have managed to capture his eye, make sure to make yourself as interesting as possible. The more of a challenge you are, the more interested he gets. However, don't overdo it – never play hard to get!

Spark his curiosity. Tell him about something interesting you've experienced and unusual places you've visited.

Listen. Allow him to elaborate on his views and dreams.

Try something new. Suggest having dinner in a lively restaurant, and introduce him to new flavours and exotic dishes. Suggest taking a day off and take off somewhere.

Positive vibes. He wants a woman to bring out the sunshine and someone who will support his plans and ideas.

Whatever you do...

- **DON'T** disclose too much too soon; leave him guessing.

- **DON'T** make him feel cornered.

- **DON'T** use rough language.

- **DON'T** fuss about money.

- **DON'T** rely on your looks alone; keep your mind sharp.

Remember, although he may be frank and outspoken, he doesn't handle "the truth" too well.

- **DON'T** leave everything up to him; show some initiative.

- **DON'T** bombard him with negativity and criticize his views.

- **DON'T** whine and complain.

- **DON'T** restrict his freedom.

- **DON'T** tell him how to run his life – or try to run it for him.

Be gentle – this guy is easily hurt and offended.

Signs you're in - or not

This is usually very easy to figure out. This man can't be bothered to spend time with people who don't inspire him – and that applies very much to women as well. If he doesn't like you, you'll know! However, if he's still around, he could be romantically interested, or not... He is a social butterfly and sometimes he includes women he meets in his extensive circle of acquaintances without going further. Women are an important part of his world, not only as romantic and erotic partners but as friends and buddies. Although this guy is impulsive, energetic and usually all over the place, there are signs you may have triggered something within him:

Chances are he will...

- call you, texts you and is generally very assertive
- give you genuine compliments
- pick gifts that mean something to you
- remember little things you've said
- clearly show his admiration for you in public
- be considerate, protective and shows himself as a true gentleman

Not your type? Making an exit

It won't take long to get rid of Mr. Sagittarius. Chances are he'll probably be out of your life before you get a chance to say goodbye. He knows instinctively how people feel – unless he decides to ignore it. This man will not be in a relationship with a woman he's not on a wavelength with, and certainly not a woman who has lost interest in him. Life is an adventure, so why waste it on a love affair which isn't going anywhere? However, if he has fallen for you and lost grip on reality, he may need a slight push to get out of your life.

Foolproof exit measures:

These measures will require you to be firm and stand your ground – and look really bad. Sometimes a firm approach is better than no approach at all – but it will be doing both of you a favour. Make sure you really want to end it before you go ahead...

- Tell him not to stay out late and to call you at a certain time so you can check on him.
- Give him the third degree when he's going out with friends: Who are you seeing? Where are you going? Will there be women there? You never told me about these women before... etc.
- Get on his back for being messy, and keep nagging till he starts cleaning up.
- Cancel a trip he's been looking forward to.
- Criticize him publicly when you're out with friends.
- When you're out, make excuses on his behalf – even when there's no need to.

CHAPTER 3

SEX'N STUFF

Seductive moves:
How to get him in the mood:

He is turned on by the chase. The excitement and uncertainty... not knowing whether he's going to succeed in seducing her or not... make him tremble with erotic passion. A woman who crosses her legs and allows her skirt to slide up a bit can make him start breathing heavily. If the woman caresses her thigh at the same time, Mr. Sagittarius may break out in a sweat.

Preferences and erotic nature

He is turned on by women's legs, especially if she is wearing sexy stockings. Another thing that gives him a great erotic kick is rubbing himself against his partner – or any woman, for that matter... If the two of you are standing in a queue and you suddenly feel your Sagittarius partner pressing his lower body against yours, you may prepare yourself for an erotic treat.

Less is more for this guy. Don't be too obvious about your intentions. If your attitude, and your outfit, is a bit too revealing, you risk turning him off. Anything vulgar is a no-no. If you manage to take it slow and use your body language in a subtle way, it won't take long before he'll be passionate about getting closer to you.

Hitting the right buttons

Although every sign has areas on the body that are more sensitive than others, individual sensitivity may vary quite a bit. Don't go body-blind. Honing in on these erogenous zones and forgetting the rest of him is not a good idea. Use these areas to create sparks while turning him on, and as a passion-booster when things get heated. Watch his body language – including the most obvious of signs. Open your mind to the sensuality of touch and taste.

Key areas
Hips and thighs

Get it on
If you want to bring out the erotic sparkle in his eyes, focus your attention on the area covering hips and thighs. There are numerous ways of arousing this guy. For instance, if the two of you are out dancing, make sure your hands touch his hips all through the slow-dance. If the dance is really slow, press your thighs against his and just watch how he brightens up.

Arouse him
In private, suggest giving him a nice oil-massage – with a focus on hips and thighs, of course. Although your touch may be gentle, chances are the massage will be far from relaxing for Mr. Sagittarius. Your partner will gradually get pretty hot inside, and it won't take long before your innocent massage has developed into a more erotic activity… If you really want him to go crazy with passion, use your tongue on his upper and inner thigh area.

Surprise him
Take the initiative when you're out in public. Do something unexpected, but only for a brief moment, like accidentally brushing your hand over his more sensitive parts, making him wonder whether you did it on purpose – or not... He loves women who manage to create excitement and suspense.

Spice it up
Roleplaying might sound a bit boring – but not so with this guy! Take on a "hello, stranger!" attitude, without telling him what you're up to ... Notice how he starts playing along. Be a little sassy about it.

Remember: When he's in the mood, he's *not* in the mood for waiting. A partner who needs to do the laundry first turns him off.

His expectations

Softness and sensuality. Femininity is the essence. Aggressiveness turns him off. Sexy underwear is a plus, providing it's not tacky. Don't forget the stockings – this guy gets a real kick from women's legs.

Make it sassy. He loves variation. If you're being too conservative or a creature of habit, you won't ring his bells.

Give and take. Traditional positions are okay, providing he gets to explore the more exotic sides of sex.

Inspire him. He appreciates new impulses and will appreciate input from you. Either tell him about previous experiences, and do a little research.

The perfect balance. He's very flexible, but his partner mustn't be too demanding – that wears him out. However, she mustn't be too passive – that bores him. His ideal encounter is a balanced energy, which demands attention from his partner.

Erotic guidance. An inexperienced woman doesn't need to worry. Mr. Sagittarius doesn't mind leading the way. He may come across as a little blunt and direct at times, but don't get offended. His goal is to please you.

Your sensual preferences
Quiz yourself and find out whether this man is for you.

Where on the scale are you?
1 = Don't agree | 3 = Sure | 5 = Agree!

1. Sex is a journey through erotic adventures. There's always something new to explore.
One a scale for 1 to 5, you are: 1 - 2 - 3- 4 - 5

2. When you're hot, you're hot! Seizing the erotic moment is important.
One a scale for 1 to 5, you are: 1 - 2 - 3- 4 - 5

3. Dragging things out is unnatural. Foreplay and intercourse should develop at their own pace.
One a scale for 1 to 5, you are: 1 - 2 - 3- 4 - 5

4. Exploring each other's bodies is an important part of sex.
One a scale for 1 to 5, you are: 1 - 2 - 3- 4 - 5

Score 15–20: Your sex life will be filled with impulsiveness, fun and desire. Enjoy!
Score 10–14: He will surprise you with energy, creativity and spontaneity. Sex will never be boring with this man.
Score 5–9: You may have mixed feelings about his sudden erotic advances, but he will probably manage to dazzle you…
Score 1–4: Sometimes you wish he could take it a little slow. Tell him, because he is very eager to please you.

CHAPTER 4

GENERAL STUFF

The big picture

Keep in mind that the characteristics of a Sagittarius may vary quite a bit depending on where within the sign he was born, as well as a wide range of additional astrological factors. But for now, let's stick to the basics. Just remember: don't jump to conclusions as soon as you meet him. Give him room to shine. Get to know the man behind the sign.

His personality: Pros and cons

Pros
- Honest and outspoken
- Has boyish charm
- Positive and energetic
- Kind
- Intelligent
- Is an attentive lover
- Is present in the moment
- Optimistic
- Lives by his own rules
- Eloquent
- Loves pondering about issues
- Knowledgeable
- Entertaining
- Social and open-minded

Cons
- Insensitive
- Childish
- Sulks if he doesn't get his way
- Weary of romantic commitment
- Absentminded
- Ignores problems
- Shuns routines
- Postpones boring tasks
- Is a sore loser
- Sarcastic
- Arrogant
- Restless and impatient
- Blunt
- Provoking

Tip: How to show romantic interest

With attentiveness, enthusiasm, support and joy. He loves being surrounded by positive energy. Show admiration for him as a man as well, and he will be convinced that you like him – a lot.

Romantic Vibes

Mr Sagittarius: The adventurous and protective partner

The essence

Embracing life. He doesn't spend every minute on the couch with his woman. Sometimes it can even be a little difficult to get him to yourself. He's always got something going on. A new idea, interesting people to see, friends to keep up with…

The true romantic. No matter how many failed relationships he has left behind, he firmly believes in 'The One', a feeling he stays with him every time he enters a relationship. "This is it, this is the woman!" If she turns out to be nothing more than a faded fantasy, he'll take off and start searching for his romantic dream elsewhere.

Freedom bonds. If his partner is just as alive and enthusiastic as him, he will carry her through life and be incredibly attentive, kind, generous and a perfect gentleman. However, if she turns out to be possessive, she better prepare herself for sarcasm and sharp remarks.

Genuine feelings. The essence of his romantic side is truthfulness. If he feels that the woman is worthy of his love, he will strive hard to make her happy, protect her, surprise her and treat her very much like a queen.

Tip: How to show erotic interest

A gentle touch on his arm, a seductive glance and a smile are usually all it takes. He's got a sixth sense when it comes to these things. Don't come on too strong, that will put him off.

Erotic Vibrations

Mr Sagittarius:
The playful and energetic lover

The essence

Erotic explorer. This is not a fiercely intense lover. He loves the quiet beauty of sex and enjoys exploring his partner's body. However, this doesn't mean that he goes on forever. He's quite impatient and eager to move on from one stage to the next.

Inspiration and creativity. Variation is important to him. Don't worry about showing off previous experience; he'd like that – providing you don't start talking about previous lovers.

A lover and a chaser. Very few men born under the sign of Sagittarius suffer from lack of sexual experience. However, he doesn't chase women for the sake of it. He's simply in love with love and will pursue it whenever he can. This may result in quite a few erotic relationships.

Persuasive. If you feel reluctant about having sex, you won't remain reluctant for long. This guy has persuasive powers bordering on the occult! He can probably talk you into doing things you previously regarded as way out of line – and chances are that you will enjoy it very much as well!

Magic hands. He has wonderful hands and knows exactly how to stimulate his partner. A sensual massage will never feel the same after having experienced Mr. Sagittarius. He can drive a woman nuts by simply using his fingertips…

CHAPTER 5

COMPATIBILITY QUIZ

Are you banging your head against the wall, or does he unleash your positive potential? Do you provoke him or bring out the best in him? Does he make you throw your arms up in exasperation, or do you feel inspired and complete in his company? Are the two of you headed towards doom or dream? Take the test to find out.

Question 1.
Do you enjoy an intense partner?

A. Sure. Sex without passion is a waste of time.
B. Not necessarily. Emotional closeness is just as important.
C. No, I don't like sweaty sex marathons! I prefer a gentle and playful approach.

Question 2.
Do you find it easy to express joy as well as giving people compliments?

A. Depends on my mood, but I'm usually pretty positive.
B. Sure! If you feel good – share it!
C. I'm no "blah-blah-space-cadet." A healthy dose of realism prevents the world from falling apart.

(cont.)

Question 3.
New ideas, impulsiveness, enthusiasm ... How do these fit into your world?

A. Very important. They're forces that drive us. I love being surrounded by enthusiastic people.
B. Sure, they're important – but it's equally important to keep your feet on the ground.
C. I wish I could be a little more enthusiastic, it's just a little difficult at times.

Question 4.
Do you enjoy your own company?

A. Not really. I tend to get bored easily. I need a guy around to keep me company.
B. Yes, I don't mind doing things on my own. Besides, enjoying my own company doesn't mean being on my own.
C. Yes, personal space is important – but if I'm in a relationship, I'd like my guy to be present.

Question 5.
Are you easily freaked out when stressed?

A. That depends on the situation. If I can't do anything about it, there's no point freaking out.
B. Yes. I hate being stressed; that's why I always make plans.
C. No problem. I'm laid back about most things. A little too much at times.

Question 6.
Does a frank and outspoken guy appeal to you?

A. I prefer a guy who thinks before he speaks. Diplomacy makes the world go around.
B. Absolutely! A guy like that will never leave me wondering about his true feelings.
C. Honesty is important, but honesty can hurt. It depends on his attitude.

Question 7.
Are you a slow mover or do you regard yourself as energetic and impatient?

A. There's nothing wrong with taking your time. It's better to do things thoroughly than making a bummer later.
B. I'm impatient by nature! What's the point of hanging around if something needs to be done or checked out?
C. A little bit of both, really. It's ok to have your head in the clouds, providing your feet touch the ground.

Question 8.
Do you enjoy traveling?

A. Yes, and it doesn't have to be far. I can get a kick from a weekend trip or even exploring a new neighbourhood in my own city.
B. Not really. People who need to experience something new 24/7 wear me out.
C. Yes, but not just for the sake of it – there must be some kind of plan or idea behind it.

Question 9.
What do you prefer? Playfulness and boyish charm or strength and masculinity?

A. I must admit, I've got a weakness for strong alpha-male types.
B. I love boyish charm. Life never gets boring with a guy like that.
C. A little bit of both, actually.

Question 10.
Do you enjoy making suggestions while having sex?

A. Sex is about communication – and there are lots of different ways to communicate.
B. No, I just do what feels right. And besides, I'm a little shy when it comes to talking about my preferences in bed.
C. Absolutely. This can open the door to new and amazing sensations!

SCORE	A	B	C
Question 1	1	5	10
Question 2	5	10	1
Question 3	10	5	1
Question 4	1	5	10
Question 5	5	1	10
Question 6	1	10	5
Question 7	1	10	5
Question 8	10	1	5
Question 9	1	10	5
Question 10	5	1	10

75 – 100
Don't be surprised if you discover he's not the man you fell in love with – but someone who's turned into someone who is so much better. You ponder about how this is possible, but most things are possible when it comes to this man. He makes you feel loved, free and liberated – a unique combination. He enriches your life in so many ways and stimulates your mind. He makes you view life from angles you probably didn't know existed. The two of you complement each other perfectly and turn life into an adventure. Enjoy!

51 – 74
Having Mr. Sagittarius around is like having an endless supply of adventures brought into your life. No days are the same. He'll surprise you with fun suggestions and exciting ideas, and there's always something going on. Sometimes it might get a tad hectic, and you might long for time together – just the two of you. He doesn't mind that at all, providing you don't get stuck in front of the TV all weekend. Come up with a few ideas. How about having fun making a new and exotic dish… or doing some yoga in the bedroom? Flexibility is very important to keep the relationship going, which shouldn't be a problem for the two of you.

26 – 50

He came into your life like a refreshing breeze with scents from a new and exotic world, but chances are that you're beginning to feel the draft and are itching to close the window. Too much excitement, no planning, constant activity... sometimes it feels like having a kid around! That's one of the aspects that makes him exciting, but also a little draining. Thoughtless comments and ignorance are the flipside of his personality. Love conquers all, and if you still feel strongly about him, these are minor obstacles that you can work through. However, turn it around. Do you feel you're able to satisfy his needs or do you expect him to adjust to yours? Think about it... You can still have a good relationship, but that requires a bit of work and commitment from both of you. Are you ready for a challenge?

10 – 25

Do something before it's too late. Make sure to save the friendship even though you're not destined to be romantic partners. If you leave it too long, hoping for a miracle, negative feelings will probably make you feel miserable. We all have different needs. You and Mr. Sagittarius are wired slightly differently and get a kick out of the opposite things – which is hardly the perfect platform to build a relationship. You may have found each other exciting, but in the long run, you'll probably end up draining each other of energy. Hold on to the positive feelings – hold on to the friendship. Your perfect romantic partners are probably waiting elsewhere.

Thoughts...
Just because you disagree on certain topics, doesn't mean you cannot have a great relationship. Sometimes we need a little resistance in order to expand our vision.

CAPRICORN the male

YOUR DATE: CAPRICORN
22 December–19 January

The Essence of him

Ambitious – outgoing – friendly – persistent – extremely goal oriented – perseverant – believes in hard work without shortcuts – diplomatic – fair and just – cuts through details and gets to the chore – objective and down-to-earth – good with money – loves luxury and quality – carefully optimistic – an excellent host and entertaining guest – loyal – reliable and dependable – intelligent

…and remember: This man will always reach his goals – if he puts his mind to it. Don't rush him. He needs to figure things out and move ahead at his own pace.

Blind Date – speedy essentials

Who's waiting for you?
You probably won't notice him right away: the classily dressed man standing towards the side of the room. He is glancing at everyone who comes through the door without being obvious about it or drawing attention to himself. This man is a master when it comes to observing. If you decided to have a few drinks before meeting him and enter the restaurant slightly tipsy and with your outfit messed up, he'll probably turn around and ignore you. This guy will not go out with a woman who doesn't meet his standards.

Emergency fixes for embarrassing pauses
Even though he may come across as masculine and outgoing, he will expect you to play an active part in the conversation – not only because he wants to check you out, but also because men born under this sign can be a little shy at times. If the conversation feels a little slow, take the initiative to talk about topics you know something about. He will appreciate a woman with her own opinions.

Your place or mine?
Sex on the first date? Very unlikely. Sex is something he saves – usually – until he has captured a woman he is romantically interested in. However, there are exceptions. He may want to join you at your place if he's afraid of losing the chance of getting to know you further. But if you really like him, it's better to save the erotic invitations until later. A little patience now can bring you loads of passion later.

Checklist, before you dash out to meet him:
Don't be late
(hint: Avoid keeping him waiting)
Look stylish from head to toe
(hint: No cheap imitations)
Don't pre-drink with girlfriends
(hint: Giggly and slightly tipsy is a no-no)
Brush up on a few topics you're interested in
(hint: He appreciates a smart woman)
Check out some places you could go
(hint: A cool bar or even a special exhibition)

Tip: Don't get too creative. This is a cool, conservative and determined man. Go for classy rather than sassy, both when it comes to appearance and approach.

CHAPTER 1

PREPARE YOURSELF

Catch his eye, capture his attention
Top 10 attention grabbers

1. Be classy. No flashy outfits.
2. Carry yourself with poise – and keep a playful sparkle in your eyes.
3. Show interest in what he's doing and what he has done before.
4. Be open and genuine in your approach.
5. Ask questions, and be smart about it.
6. Admire him, but only if it's called for and he deserves it. No fake compliments!
7. Be cheerful, optimistic and outgoing.
8. Show him that you have an independent mind and your own opinions.
9. Be flexible in your views, but don't compromise your own opinions.
10. Let him know that you appreciate a man being a man.

The SHE. The woman!

The Capricorn male regards himself as a true man, in the traditional sense of the word: strong, reliable and masculine. His partner must be able to appreciate these qualities in order to enjoy him. His perfect woman does not compete with him, but rather makes the picture complete. She is independent and intelligent, but never aggressive or pushy. She is feminine, but never girly and giggly. She is cool, classy – and his feminine reflection.

The Essence of her

Feminine – intelligent – cheerful – attractive – appreciates masculinity and the strength of a man – well-mannered – enjoys chivalrous attention – carries herself like a woman – independent – supportive – loyal – optimistic – encouraging when days are grey – shows respect and admiration for her partner's efforts, both at work and in their personal life – applauds his ambition

---

Capricorn arousal meter

From 0 to 100... One hour – or one year! The Capricorn man is extremely patient, and he can hold back until he has captured his woman...

Remember: Be true to yourself
It doesn't matter if he is the most stunning guy you've ever met – if you don't match, you don't match. You may be able to put on a show for a while to hold his attention, but what's the point? We can't please everybody. We all have different needs, dreams, tastes and preferences. There's no such thing as a one-size-fits-all lover. Be yourself, and be true to who you are – always!

Very important: Don't be too fixed in your ways. Flexibility is the key to getting on with this guy. When he's stubborn, go for a diplomatic approach.

CHAPTER 2

THE FIRST DATE

Getting your foot in the door
The basics

Femininity rules. Your attitude is very important. If you find it difficult to live out your feminine side and allow a man to be a man, you may have a problem.

Be attentive. As soon as you've got his attention, be attentive, listen and ask questions.

Genuine admiration. Feel free to admire him and pay him compliments, but only do so genuinely. Never feign positive attention with this guy.

Trigger his curiosity. There must be something about you that sparks his interest – something that isn't too obvious. This could be a discreet, playful glance, perhaps, or a feminine outfit ... anything that triggers his subconscious desire.

Stand on your own feet. Being smart and independent is always a great plus – provided there is still plenty of room for a masculine male in your life.

Grace and flexibility. He appreciates an easygoing woman who knows how to carry herself. Rigid women drive him nuts.

Whatever you do...

- **DON'T** interrupt him or disagree loudly.

- **DON'T** use crude language.

- **DON'T** express a negative outlook on life.

- **DON'T** be hyper-positive and out-of-touch with reality.

- **DON'T** pretend to know more about a topic than you do.

Remember, There are no shortcuts to his heart. Even if he is interested in you, feelings need to

- **DON'T** wear anything eye-popping, even if it's fashionable.

- **DON'T** serve him white lies in order to impress him.

- **DON'T** be sexually aggressive.

- **DON'T** criticize him when he's being gallant.

- **DON'T** forget your manners. Mind what you say and do.

develop naturally. Don't push him. Be patient.

Signs you're in - or not

Love at first sight is not really the Capricorn man's thing. He is far too analytical to allow himself to get carried away by feelings that haven't had a chance to develop naturally. However, he will observe you closely, and if he feels the two of you may have more potential than a nice evening, he will pursue you. If you have made a thorough impression on him, he will probably be quite persistent in his approach. When he's on to something good, there's only one option: success. The following are some clear indications that he's got his eyes on you:

Chances are he will...

- call or text you the next day
- suggest going out very soon after your first date
- pamper you in an old-fashioned way: flowers, dinner, etc.
- be attentive and help you with personal or professional tasks
- share his personal views and ideas with you
- act protective when you are around other guys

Not your type? Making an exit

The Capricorn man is practical in all areas of life, including his love life. If things are not working out, he'll talk to you about it and try to figure something out. If there's nothing more to build on, he will suggest moving on. Being stuck in a relationship is not his thing. He needs to have a purpose in everything he does. Everything must be growing and moving

moving forward. Love is a living thing. If it's withering, he will find more nourishing soil.

However, there are Capricorns who refuse to see what's going on and who insist on making it work, because if you put your mind to it, it will ... right? These men need to be kicked out of their comfort zone. Forcing them to touch base with reality can actually help them move forward and thrive.

Foolproof exit measures:

These strategies will make you look like an idiot. But if that's what it takes to send him out of your life, well ... that's what it takes!

- Be crude in language and appearance
- Insist that he spend more time with you than on his interests
- Tell silly jokes in bed and give the impression that sex is purely a physical thing
- Start throwing your money around
- Criticize him for being polite and attentive, saying that this isn't the 1950s
- Pick arguments whenever you can and disagree loudly

CHAPTER 3

SEX'N STUFF

Seductive moves:
How to get him in the mood:

It is your mind, not the size of your bra, that will spark his erotic interest. Combine your alert mind with closeness and intimacy, and he will start to ease into sensual feelings. A seductive glance can do more for him than any other man in the zodiac. Add a bit of slow, seductive dancing and he'll be ready to go.

Preferences and erotic nature

The Capricorn man will always make an effort, and he expects his woman to do the same. In order to make him happy, you should always pay close attention to what he enjoys in bed. Remember the details, and introduce them next time you have sex with him. He can go all night without tiring, and he has a unique ability to satisfy his partner. Forget acrobatic stunts: he believes in the quiet and intense pleasures of sex and prefers them in comfortable surroundings – not in the backseat of a car! No matter how much you try to persuade him, this man won't let his trousers drop until he feels comfortable. Never, ever try to tell him what to do. He's got firm opinions about sex and won't allow himself to be pushed into something he's not comfortable with.

Hitting the right buttons

Although every sign has areas on the body that are more sensitive than others, individual sensitivity may vary quite a bit. Don't go body-blind. Honing in on these erogenous zones and forgetting the rest of him is not a good idea. Use these areas to create sparks while turning him on, and as a passion-booster when things get heated. Watch his body language – including the most obvious of signs. Open your mind to the sensuality of touch and taste.

Key areas
The entire back

Get it on
If he asks you to give him a backrub, be careful and aware of what you are doing, because his erogenous zone is his back! If you're not in the mood for sex, you need to make sure the massage resembles a rough physiotherapy treatment.

Arouse him
On the other hand, if you want to experience the erotic side of him, be gentle with your massage – very gentle. Apply oil or cream to facilitate smooth movement over his back. Let your hands brush over his buttocks, lower back and sides, but be careful not to tickle him. What may put other guys to sleep will have the opposite effect on him.

Surprise him
Put on some slow music and start unbuttoning his shirt while the two of you are dancing. This should spark his interest. Continue dancing on your own while slowly stripping all your clothes off.

Spice it up
Take the backrub a bit further. Gently apply some whipped cream or sweet liqueur to his back and playfully lick it off.

Remember: Although he is a strong and confident lover, he relies heavily on feedback from his partner during sex. Let him know how you feel.

His expectations

No erotic expeditions. His ideal woman mustn't be too demanding or adventurous. If sex is turned into some kind of erotic expedition with little closeness or sensitivity, he'll lose interest.

Be present, be active. She must be feminine, tender and actively participating. A date who leaves everything to him won't get a second chance. In fact, he can be offended by a passive partner.

No cheeky stuff. The atmosphere needs to be right, and the surroundings comfortable. Don't suggest a quick one in an unusual place. This is not his thing.

Sensual guidance. He doesn't expect his partner to be an erotic expert. He is more than willing to teach, inspire and guide an inexperienced woman, which can be a great boost to the relationship.

Nourish his masculinity. He enjoys a woman who truly appreciates his masculinity. The appreciation will make him even more eager to please her.

Time and place. If he's not in the mood, he's not in the mood! If he's got too much going on in his mind, he won't be able to free his body and relax.

Your sensual preferences
Quiz yourself and find out whether this man is for you.

Where on the scale are you?
1 = Don't agree | 3 = Sure | 5 = Agree!

1. Comfortable and private surroundings are important for enjoying sex.
One a scale for 1 to 5, you are: 1 - 2 - 3- 4 - 5

2. Erotic acrobatics are distracting and diminish pleasure.
One a scale for 1 to 5, you are: 1 - 2 - 3- 4 - 5

3. Intimacy and chemistry do more for passion than sex toys.
One a scale for 1 to 5, you are: 1 - 2 - 3- 4 - 5

4. Atmosphere is very important for creating a sensual mood.
One a scale for 1 to 5, you are: 1 - 2 - 3- 4 - 5

Score 15–20: The two of you are incredibly attuned to each other. There will be a lot of pleasure ahead.
Score 10–14: Sex with him might be a little slower and more intense than what you're used to, but the pleasure and satisfaction will probably be amazing.
Score 5–9: It's very important to communicate – otherwise, the two of you might lose out on significant pleasure. Get to know each other's preferences. Don't be afraid to ask.
Score 1–4: You may be a little too restless to enjoy this man as a lover. Slowing down could broaden your horizons. Try it.

CHAPTER 4

GENERAL STUFF

The big picture

Keep in mind that the characteristics of a Capricorn may vary quite a bit depending on where within the sign he was born, as well as a wide range of additional astrological factors. But for now, let's stick to the basics. Just remember: don't jump to conclusions as soon as you meet him. Give him room to shine. Get to know the man behind the sign.

His personality: Pros and cons

Pros
- Attentive
- Charming
- Thorough
- Persistent
- Loyal
- Confident and friendly
- Grounded and controlled
- Optimistic
- A born leader
- Trustworthy
- Classy and stylish
- Intelligent
- Patient
- An excellent host

Cons
- Chauvinistic
- Traditional
- Conservative
- A slow mover
- A lone wolf
- Snobbish
- Stubborn
- Self-centred
- Fixed in his views
- Critical
- Inflexible
- Controlling
- Judgmental
- Has high expectations

Tip: How to show romantic interest

Show genuine admiration for him. Be supportive of his ideas. Do something that shows our effort, like making him his dinner or suggesting an activity based on something you know he's interested in.

Romantic Vibes

Mr Capricorn:
The strong and chivalrous partner

The essence

A lone rider. He may come across as a guy who can move through life perfectly well on his own – and he probably could. However, he prefers to have a woman by his side.

True love. His partner needs to provide love, support and inspiration; she will give him the affirmation he needs.

No time wasters, please. He doesn't throw his love around and is prepared to take his time searching for the woman of his dreams.

Loving actions. He sometimes finds it difficult to express his feelings with words, and his partner needs to know how to interpret actions that signal his love.

Enjoy time together. He is attentive, loving and caring. It's not his style to spend the evenings out on the town with his friends. When he has found a woman he truly cares about, he will want to spend time with her.

…but pursue interests separately. It's important to him to be able to pursue hobbies and interests individually. This can enrich the relationship and make the bond stronger.

No quitter. He will never leave at the first sight of friction. He will stay and try his best to work things out.

Tip: How to show erotic interest

Get closer to him physically, without being obvious about it. Establish closeness when you're out walking or dancing. But be careful not to come across as clingy – that will turn him off.

Erotic Vibrations

Mr Capricorn:
The intense and determined lover

The essence

No demanding sexual athlete. He doesn't seek erotic fulfillment whenever possible. The interest is there, but it's seldom imposing.

Quiet beauty of sex. He's not into erotic acrobatics or wild nights. This guy prefers the quiet beauty of sex: closeness, intimacy and tenderness. But this doesn't mean he's not passionate. He is sensual, highly erotic and difficult to resist.

Mindful sensuality. For him, sex is seldom about pure physical satisfaction. The emotional side is just as important.

Sensual emotions. Words of love don't come naturally to him, and he often prefers to show his feelings during sex. This can make the sensual moments very intense and tender.

Erotic thermostat. He needs to let the erotic temperature develop naturally.

Stamina. He's not the most sexually creative guy in the zodiac, but he makes up for it with intensity and endurance.

Brings out the best in her. He has a unique ability to make his woman feel like a naughty princess in bed, regardless of how much experience she may or may not have.

CHAPTER 5

COMPATIBILITY QUIZ

───────────────

Are you banging your head against the wall, or does he unleash your positive potential? Do you provoke him or bring out the best in him? Does he make you throw your arms up in exasperation, or do you feel inspired and complete in his company? Are the two of you headed towards doom or dream? Take the test to find out.

Question 1.
Is it important to you that your partner express his feelings with words?

A. I'm not particular about how he does it, as long as he manages to his feelings in one way or another.
B. Of course. How else am I supposed to know how he feels?
C. Not really, but sometimes it's nice to hear sweet nothings.

Question 2.
What male personality do you find it easiest to connect with?

A. Someone who's playful and boyish.
B. A stylish and passionate guy.
C. A persistent and ambitious type.

(cont.)

Question 3.
Do you enjoy having sex in new and unusual places, or do you prefer comfortable surroundings?

A. I prefer comfortable and romantic settings.
B. Traditional lovemaking is not my style. I enjoy new experiences, including new places to have sex.
C. Although I've been dreaming about sex on the beach in the moonlight, I tend toward comfortable surroundings in real life.

Question 4.
Do you consider yourself goal-oriented and persistent?

A. Sometimes. It depends on how important the goal is to me.
B. Yes. Setting goals is the first step to success.
C. Not really. I don't have the patience.

Question 5.
Do you think it's important to express love during sex?

A. Yes, but it all depends on the mood. Sometimes I just want a bit of passion.
B. Yes, absolutely. It can elevate the pleasure to new heights.
C. Sex and love are two different things. Why try to mix them?

Question 6.
What does it take to get you in the mood?

A. An expensive gift.
B. A few tender words whispered into your ear.
C. A nice dinner at an intimate restaurant.

Question 7.
How would you feel if a nice guy showed interest in you – and was very persistent about it?

A. I'd love it. It would make me feel desired.
B. Annoyed. I can't stand pushy guys.
C. I don't know. It would depend on whether I really liked him or not.

Question 8.
Do you find it easy to adjust to new situations?

A. Usually it's no problem.
B. Not really. I'm pretty set in my ways.
C. It all depends. If I have met a really nice man, I can be pretty flexible.

Question 9.
Does material success mean a lot to you?

A. Not at all. There are many more important things in life.
B. Yes. It's a reward for working hard and striving towards your goals.
C. Yes, but I'm not completely fixated on it.

Question 10.
Do you mind if your man pursues interests on his own?

A. It's fine, provided he's not away every night or every weekend.
B. No. It's important to do things together. It will make the relationship more rewarding.
C. Yes! What's the point having a relationship if we're not doing things together?

SCORE	A	B	C
Question 1	10	1	5
Question 2	1	5	10
Question 3	10	1	5
Question 4	5	10	1
Question 5	5	10	1
Question 6	1	5	10
Question 7	10	1	5
Question 8	10	1	5
Question 9	1	10	5
Question 10	5	10	1

75 – 100
The two of you make a power duo in every aspect of life. You inspire and support each other. You communicate with minimal misunderstandings. You share love and affection on a unique level, and your feelings are expressed through everything you do – and no matter what you choose to do, you make a perfect team. This special relationship has the potential to grow and become stronger throughout life. You have managed to become friends, partners and lovers: a true recipe for happiness.

51 – 74
You probably know it already – but this feels good. You admire his drive and strength; he cherishes your enthusiasm, support and loyalty. You bring that extra spark to his life, and he makes sure your life is safe and comfortable. Sure, there will be a few lively discussions from time to time, but they will prevent the relationship from becoming boring. You share a mutual respect and are able to inspire each other. Sometimes you don't even have to say anything; the things you do will spark ideas and creativity. Enjoy!

26 – 50
Love is not always a walk in the park, and sometimes achieving happiness and fulfillment requires effort. You may find yourself debating quite a few things in this relationship. Even though you love him, certain elements of his personality drive you nuts from time to time, especially when he's being extremely focused and persistent. Sometimes you wish he'd be a little more playful and spontaneous, –not so serious about life all the time. He makes you feel safe and desired, but what about your happiness? You need to figure out what's important to you and whether he fits into your life. Keep in mind that a life worth having is worth fighting for – no matter if he's there or not.

10 – 25
If you don't leave, he probably will – and that says a lot, because this man is not a quitter. At this point, you need to figure out what you're doing: are you spending time together or wasting time together? If you don't have anything to offer each other besides irritation and negative vibes, it's time to move on. Don't let pride get in the way. Cutting through when things are not working is not a failure; it's constructive and productive. Both of you need to thrive, and the best way to do this is to define your values, follow your heart and move on.

Thoughts...
If you really want something. If you feel it's right. If you know it'll be difficult - but worth it... Go for it!

Sometimes, making an effort makes the reward much more satisfying.

AQUARIUS the male

YOUR DATE: AQUARIUS
20 January – 18 February

The Essence of him

A true individualist – spontaneous – colourful – checks out new things – shows genuine interest – loves to figure things out – intrigued by the human mind – no problem acquiring wisdom and knowledge from others – not impressed by titles or money – seeks truth and knowledge – strong intuition – emotionally detached – loves to stand out – self-disciplined – does not conform

…and remember: He won't enter into close friendships before he is certain about people's intentions. Earning his trust takes time.

Blind Date – speedy essentials

Who's waiting for you?
No one, because he will probably be late. He has 1000 things going in his mind and is easily distracted when something captures his interest. After having waited ten minutes or so, keep an eye out for a guy who sticks out in one way or another – maybe a slightly unusual hairstyle or piece of clothing. He will approach you as a friend and start talking about something interesting he's been thinking about. Remember, you are on a date with the individualist of the zodiac. Anything can happen. Prepare yourself for all sorts of spontaneous and weird conversations.

Emergency fixes for embarrassing pauses
If he likes you, he will always come up with something to talk about – even though it may not interest you all that much. His social antenna can be a little off-base at times. Should he run out of topics, which is very unlikely, go ahead and fill in. Talk about anything from music to the occult, but make sure to show some depth. This man can't stand superficial people.

Your place or mine?
Sex on the first date? No problem. If you hit it off, he won't mind joining you back at home to share a bottle wine or a some exotic snacks. He is very much an adventurer. A new partner represents new turf for him to explore. He is not a naturally passionate guy, and the erotic feelings will take time to develop – provided he feels inspired. You may end up spending the night talking instead.

Checklist, before you dash out to meet him:
Bring a small, unusual gift or surprise
(hint: Make it very special)
Wear a piece of jewelery that stands out
(hint: Make him curious)
Check out new restaurants ahead of time
(hint: He'd love something new)
Have some interesting knowledge ready to share
(hint: He loves to explore and learn)
Be prepared to raise a few erotic ideas
(hint: Make it exotic, but not crude)

Tip: He will welcome anything that can broaden his horizon, especially if it's a little out of the ordinary. This applies to his sex life as well – but avoid anything vulgar.

CHAPTER 1

PREPARE YOURSELF

Catch his eye, capture his attention
Top 10 attention grabbers

1. Take the initiative, but be subtle.
2. Tell him about exotic places you've visited, or want to visit, and why.
3. Make sure there's something unusual about you (hair, clothing, jewelery, etc).
4. Don't reveal too much. Keep a slight aura of mystery.
5. Inspire him. He loves learning new things.
6. Don't be aggressive. Make him feel relaxed in your company.
7. Be feminine, soft and a little innocent in your demeanour.
8. Let there be something unique about you, something that makes you stand out.
9. Present him with an interesting challenge that needs to be solved.
10. Listen and ask smart questions.

The SHE. The woman!

Some may claim that this man's dream woman is almost a fantasy. His expectations are many and specific. Feminine charm is not enough: she must also be alert and intelligent, sparking his interest and making him curious about her and life in general. She needs to be soft and feminine, as well as independent and strong. His ideal woman is a free spirit who allows him to take the lead. Most importantly, she must also be his friend and companion – and an adventurous lover.

The Essence of her
Alert – flexible – independent – feminine and sweet – supportive and interested in his ideas and projects – a constant challenge and a source of inspiration – interesting, with an appetite for the mysteries of life – a free spirit – adventurous – liberated – optimistic – slightly mysterious – erotically exciting – open-minded – open to topics that are a little out of the ordinary

---

Aquarius' arousal meter
From 0 to 100... in an hour - or several days. It depends on whether it's a dawning mystery or sudden adventure.

Remember: Be true to yourself

It doesn't matter if he is the most stunning guy you've ever met – if you don't match, you don't match. You may be able to put on a show for a while to hold his attention, but what's the point? We can't please everybody. We all have different needs, dreams, tastes and preferences. There's no such thing as a one-size-fits-all lover. Be yourself, and be true to who you are – always!

Very important: Don't rush him, either in sex or romance. He needs to get to know you and feel comfortable around you, before he makes up his mind.

CHAPTER 2

THE FIRST DATE

Getting your foot in the door
The basics

Trigger his mind. Forget about dressing up in a sexy outfit. He will either look at you strangely or not notice at all. You need to appeal to his mind, not his toolbox.

Inspire him. If you manage to introduce him to new topics, people and exciting places, you'll have his attention.

Make a move. He can be quite shy, which is why he prefers a woman to make the first move. This doesn't mean you can run him over like a steamroller. Guide him gently.

Give him space. If you try to dominate him or boss him around, he'll be off.

Free your spirit. If you're really serious about him, let him know that you appreciate freedom as much as he does.

In the mood? Be smart about it. This guy isn't easily seduced. He needs to appreciate you as a person before he will become erotically involved. If you are in a hurry, tell him you need someone to teach you a thing or two. This could work - or it could result in a lecture on lovemaking.

Whatever you do...

- **DON'T** come across as aggressive or too assertive.

- **DON'T** be argumentative and fixed in your opinions.

- **DON'T** criticise others for being original.

- **DON'T** wear overly suggestive clothing.

- **DON'T** push him into making a decision.

Remember, don't reveal too much right away. Keep him guessing. He loves the suspense.

- **DON'T** make fun of his unusual ideas.

- **DON'T** ask him what kind of salary he's aiming for.

- **DON'T** keep looking at your watch, telling him that sleep is a priority.

- **DON'T** refuse to see things from new perspectives.

- **DON'T** get distracted from what he's saying.

There must be loads of room for mysteries for him to figure out. Never allow him to read you like an open book.

Signs you're in - or not

Keep in mind that a relationship with him will usually start as a friendship, and that every friendship takes a while for him to establish. However, on a rare occasion, a mysterious and interesting woman may ignite his romantic dreams and drive him to pursue her without the usual get-to-know-each-other-first phase. In that case, she'll need to live up to the vision he has created of her. Could be fun. Could be a challenge. Could be absolutely worth it! If you have managed to turn him into a romantic explorer, you will probably start to notice a thing or two...

Chances are he will...

- invite you out for an unusual meal or a drink
- suggest listening to some new music while taking a herbal bath
- keep you up late at night to explore books or movies
- change or adjust his style in order to impress you
- serve you exotic fruits or drinks
- be willing to explore erotic mysteries with you

Not your type? Making an exit

An Aquarius man will never let anything or anyone hold him back or restrict his freedom. If things are not working out, he will be off before you've even had a chance to think about it. There will be no drama – just an exit. It takes a very special woman to compel him to commit to a long-term relationship. Either it feels right, or it doesn't. He's basically looking to date a soul-mate. A fling might be fun, but it will take more than an interesting erotic adventure to keep him around.

However, if you are the one who's had enough, and he doesn't get it, he's probably far too absorbed in a project or busy turning you into a dream woman in his mind. No need to worry. Getting an Aquarius to pack his bags is easy. If you have reached this stage, you need to get his attention.

Foolproof exit measures:

There's no need to go over the top. Simple things and suggestions can make this man freak out. Here are a few examples:

- Get jealous and ask him where he has been and with whom
- Make a fuss about his mess and tell him to be tidier
- Insist on talking about feelings and make him commit to the future
- Become rigid and conservative in your views
- Get angry and upset whenever he's late - for anything
- Introduce routines to 'help him' become more efficient

CHAPTER 3

SEX'N STUFF

Seductive moves:
How to get him in the mood:

The Aquarius's mind is probably his biggest erogenous zone. You won't get far without appealing to his thoughts and fantasies. You need to present your ideas as suggestions. Allow him to visualize the possibilities and let them sink in. Make the surroundings comfortable and a little exotic. Pillows are great, and they can be handy during the erotic adventure…

Preferences and erotic nature

He is willing to try most things - once. His constant need for change applies to his sex life as well. He wants sex at different times, day and night. As far as positions are concerned, he is probably the only male in the zodiac that is capable of making the old missionary position a new adventure every time you try it. He is playful, but he seldom wastes his money on expensive sexual gadgets. He prefers to use his imagination. If he ever uses anything besides his hands and body, it's usually something natural, like oils, creams and chocolate.

Hitting the right buttons

Although every sign has areas on the body that are more sensitive than others, individual sensitivity may vary quite a bit. Don't go body-blind. Honing in on these erogenous zones and forgetting the rest of him is not a good idea. Use these areas to create sparks while turning him on, and as a passion-booster when things get heated. Watch his body language – including the most obvious of signs. Open your mind to the sensuality of touch and taste.

Key areas
Lower legs and ankles

Get it on
If you want spark his erotic interest, pay close attention to his ankles. This area works like an 'on' button, no matter whether you're at home or out in public. Playing footsie in a restaurant can take on a completely new meaning with this man. Kick off your shoes and make sure your feet are nice and soft. The fact that he's being aroused in a public place will add to the excitement.

Arouse him
If he doesn't seem all that keen on sex, it might be a good idea to give him a gentle massage, paying special attention to his feet, calves and ankles. This is usually all it takes to stir up the erotic feelings within him. Make sure to touch him gently. Being too rough will turn him off.

Surprise him

The prospect of experiencing something new is a great turn-on for an Aquarius. Tell him you're studying tantric sex (or something similar) and need someone to practice on. Give him a few hints as to what he may expect...

Spice it up

Tell him about your erotic fantasies – but only the ones you want to try out. Bring a fun erotic toy to bed and allow him to explore you.

Remember: His sex life is ruled by his mind. Sassy underwear alone won't do it. He needs something that triggers his imagination, something inspiring, tantalizing and a little mysterious...

His expectations

Prepare to say yes. He needs a partner with an open mind. More traditional women who prefer it once a week under the covers with the lights out are not his preference.

Go exploring. You don't have to be particularly experienced or creative, provided that you're eager to explore erotic pleasures.

A little creativity makes all the difference. Traditional positions are fine. He will simply try things from a new angle in order to make the sensation more exciting.

Liberate yourself. He expects to expand his sensual horizons by trying new things. Doing the same over and over again will cause him to lose interest.

Take it slow and enjoy the scenery. He loves the erotic journey and can actually be a little indifferent about climaxing – or he may turn it around completely and focus on different ways of experiencing orgasm. He can be a little either/or.

Be ready. He can come up with erotic invitations at the weirdest moments, and he will expect his partner to play along. This can either be very exiting or quite tiring, depending on your preferences.

Your sensual preferences
Quiz yourself and find out whether this man is for you.

Where on the scale are you?
1 = Don't agree | 3 = Sure | 5 = Agree!

1. Orgasm is just a bonus. The erotic journey is far more important.
One a scale for 1 to 5, you are: 1 - 2 - 3- 4 - 5

2. Exploring each other's bodies can be very satisfying.
One a scale for 1 to 5, you are: 1 - 2 - 3- 4 - 5

3. Intense passion can ruin the mysteries of sex.
One a scale for 1 to 5, you are: 1 - 2 - 3- 4 - 5

4. Sex should not be confined to certain times or places.
One a scale for 1 to 5, you are: 1 - 2 - 3- 4 - 5

Score 15–20: You truly enjoy the exotic pleasures of sex and share his need for adventure.
Score 10–14: The relationship will never be boring, and he will probably bring out your adventurous side.
Score 5–9: He wants sex to be fun, exciting and interesting; you appreciate passion and a wonderful finish. You may want to talk things over with him…
Score 1–4: The two of you are not on the same level. Looking for passion, tenderness and closeness? This is not your man.

CHAPTER 4

GENERAL STUFF

The big picture

Keep in mind that the characteristics of an Aquarius may vary quite a bit depending on where within the sign he was born, as well as a wide range of additional astrological factors. But for now, let's stick to the basics. Just remember: don't jump to conclusions as soon as you meet him. Give him room to shine. Get to know the man behind the sign.

His personality: Pros and cons

Pros
- Open to learn from others
- Genuine
- Curious
- Good listener
- Individualist
- Eloquent and convincing
- Very intuitive
- Intelligent
- Analytical
- Self-disciplined
- Unconventional
- Unafraid
- Explores and moves forward
- Creates his own destiny

Cons
- Restless
- Distracted
- Self-obsessed
- Emotionally detached
- Superficial
- Drifting
- Controlling
- Distrusting
- A lone wolf
- Prone to withdrawal
- Indecisive
- Stubborn
- Obsessed with freedom
- Intellectually snobbish

Tip: How to show romantic interest

Be supportive of his ideas. Spend time exploring his interests, and give him a special gift that shows you're paying attention and that you understand him.

Romantic Vibes

Mr Aquarius:
The independent and considerate partner

The essence

Keeping his distance… for a little while. It can be difficult to get to know him. Although he's generous and friendly, he might seem to be holding something back. This is simply because he is afraid to get too close too soon.

Love rocks, but friendship rules. Don't try pushing him into a relationship. Love usually starts with friendship. Sometimes it may seem as though he's more interested in a friend than a girlfriend – but that's just his way.

A playful soul mate. He seeks a partner who is a companion in every area of life.

Commitment and higher love. Romance is important to him, but on a different level – almost intellectual and something to explore and strive towards. When he does get romantically involved, he will devote loads of time to his partner.

Space and room to breathe. He needs freedom to make up his own mind. This is very important for the relationship to work.

No fussing, please! He doesn't like to be told when to go out, where or with whom. This will make him feel trapped and restless.

Tip: How to show erotic interest

Casually guide the conversation in an erotic direction. Ask him for his opinion and let him know that you are curious about whether something is as amazing as it seems to be...

Erotic Vibrations

Mr Aquarius:
The curious and exploring lover

The essence

A slightly unusual lover. Just when you think things are about to get a little steamy, he may start thinking about something unrelated. Suddenly the two of you may find yourselves sitting naked in bed having a lively discussion.

Seizing the erotic moment. He can be so absorbed in foreplay that he forgets about having an orgasm. To him, sex is an adventurous trip into the unknown, and sometimes the trip itself becomes more fascinating than the climax.

From dream to reality. He is not a selfish lover – far from it. He's willing to explore your fantasies and make you experience the pleasure of your erotic dreams.

Loves a challenge. He is a master when it comes to pleasing his partner. If you regard yourself as reserved, with him, you won't remain shy for long! An Aquarius man loves a challenge. Even if he can't arouse you physically, he will probably manage to do so mentally.

Spicy suggestions. Don't expect him to stick to old routines. He needs constant change and new inputs. He may suggest having sex in unusual places and in different ways – anything that may bring excitement into his sex life.

CHAPTER 5

COMPATIBILITY QUIZ

Are you banging your head against the wall, or does he unleash your positive potential? Do you provoke him or bring out the best in him? Does he make you throw your arms up in exasperation, or do you feel inspired and complete in his company? Are the two of you headed towards doom or dream? Take the test to find out.

Question 1
You wake up one morning 'in the mood'. How do you react when your partner ignores all the hints and starts talking about his plans for the day?

A. It's typical. Sometimes I wonder if he fancies me at all.
B. I would be a little upset…
C. That's just who he is. Besides, I know he will make up for it later in the day.

Question 2
Do you mind a man who sometimes gets completely absorbed in himself and his own interests?

A. Not at all. I enjoy guys who get into things.
B. Yes. I can't stand selfish dudes.
C. I don't mind – provided it's not all the time.

(cont.)

Question 3.
Do you think it's possible to get so into foreplay that you forget about an orgasm?

A. I'd like to meet a guy who's that good.
B. Yes, absolutely. Sex is more than steamy passion. It's about playfulness and exploring new sensations.
C. Absolutely not!

Question 4.
Is financial security important to you?

A. Sure, but I'm not hooked on it. As long as I'm happy with my man, I don't mind taking things as they come.
B. Financial insecurity freaks me out.
C. I'm not that good with savings, but I usually have my bills and expenses under control.

Question 5.
Do you mind telling your partner about previous sexual experiences?

A. Not at all. It could be an inspiration for both of us.
B. No, but only if he asks me.
C. Yes – that's too intimate. I like to keep certain things to myself.

Question 6.
Are you a social butterfly, or do you prefer to spend quality time with a few close friends?

A. Having people around me all the time drains me.
B. I'm very social. I love meeting new people.
C. A little bit of both, really. Depends on my mood.

Question 7.
Think about it: Why do you really want a partner?

A. I like having someone to snuggle with.
B. It's nice to have someone to share intimate things with.
C. To experience the unique combination of friendship and sensuality, and have someone bringing out the best in me.

Question 8.
What traits do you usually emphasise when trying to attract a man?

A. My personality and my feminine sides.
B. My body. I have good curves, so why not show them off?
C. My hobbies and interests. There's no point spending a lot of time getting to know a man if we don't have anything in common.

Question 9.
Do you think it's important to be mentally aroused in order to fully enjoy your partner?

A. One usually follows the other. Physical connection leads to mental connection, and the other way around.
B. Is it even possible to have sex without being mentally aroused…?
C. No. That sounds a little weird. As long as my body works, I'm good.

Question 10.
Do you think it's important to explore your erotic life?

A. Yes, I love exploring the mysteries of sex.
B. Sure, it's always fun add a bit of spice.
C. No. Sex is about intimacy and closeness – it's not a creativity contest.

SCORE	A	B	C
Question 1	1	5	10
Question 2	10	1	5
Question 3	5	10	1
Question 4	10	1	5
Question 5	10	5	1
Question 6	1	10	5
Question 7	1	5	10
Question 8	5	1	10
Question 9	5	10	1
Question 10	5	1	10

75 – 100

Wow. This is so good you might be tempted to start believing in fate. The two of you have probably discussed fate already ... or something similar. This relationship will never get boring. You will always be exploring something, inspiring each other and helping each other grow. You share the belief that love happens on a higher level, and the same applies to sex. You complement each other perfectly and love each other's company. The two of you could thrive on a deserted island. Enjoy!

51 – 74

He has entered your life and made everything come alive. Sure, he can be extremely messy and distracted, but there's something about him that helps your overlook the things that would drive other people nuts. If you want to keep him to yourself, you really have to make an effort. This guy is constantly on the move, either in the real world or in his mind. He's not really into romantic evenings – unless there's something new he wants to try; exotic candles, erotic massage or new techniques or flavours. Be flexible and tolerant, and he will bring adventures to your life.

26 – 50

Of course it can be fun to date a man who is completely different to the other guys you've met. He may impress you with knowledge and new ideas, and approach traditional topics from a new angle and turn the day upside down … but is there something missing? Do you wish you had a little more influence on the relationship? Do you get upset when he loses track of time and shows up two hours late for a date? Are you missing more tenderness and romance in your life? Chances are very slim that Mr Aquarius will change. He may try to please you for a while, but then he'll forget. It might be time to cut through. Give it a shot, but be honest with yourself.

10 – 25

This could be a fun friendship, but hardly a happy and romantic relationship. When it comes to intimacy, you disagree about most things. You set your standards, while he shrugs his shoulders. You voice your opinions, but he starts talking about an interesting album he just listened to. You can criticize as much as you like, or even show your feelings and let him know when you are hurt, but it doesn't really seem to think in. It's almost as if you are talking past each other. Yes, he may be a fun adventure, but it's time for you to start exploring happiness elsewhere.

Thoughts…
Flexibility can turn things around. Communication can open doors. A different approach to an old topic can make you see your partner in a new and colourful light.

PISCES the male

YOUR DATE: PISCES
19 February–20 March

The Essence of him

Dreamy – romantic – sensitive – creative – inquisitive – happy (seemingly) – absent-minded; loses track of time – naïvely charming – genuine – good-intentioned – spontaneous – intense and confident in bed – kind – adventurous – loves beauty –empathetic – knowledgeable – perceptive – has a good memory – unpretentious – conflict-avoidant

...and remember: He may come across as a Man – and sometimes even a toughie – but at heart, he's a big kid. It's his boyish side that draws him to strong, cheerful, smart and playful women.

Blind Date – speedy essentials

Who's waiting for you?
See the way he looks at you when you enter the room? His easy smile may give the impression that he's not taking the date seriously and that he's just doing it for kicks. Not the case! This guy's got a unique way of sparking your interest, but you won't notice this until you're hooked. He's genuinely charming, and there's nothing fake about him. Forget about the guys who've been trying to impress you with big cars, fat wallets and inflated egos. This guy really wants to get to know you – and he'll have a great time doing it.

Emergency fixes for embarrassing pauses
Don't worry, the chances of an embarrassing pause with the Pisces man are slim to none. He'll either be absorbed in whatever you're telling him or busy sharing his knowledge with you – and this guy knows a little about a lot. The only women who can manage to shut him up and send his eyes darting around the room are ones who are shallow, negative or nagging.

Your place or mine?
Sex on a first date is not typical of Mr Pisces. But if he really likes you, and both mood and situation turn passionate, he won't say no. He's got a romantic streak, so he won't suggest a quick one in the backseat of his car. But don't be fooled into thinking he's a softie. He'll drop his boyish nature along with his clothes and display himself as a true Man!

Checklist, before you dash out to meet him:
Clear your agenda – at least from early meetings
(hint: It might get late…)
Make a fun comment when you see him
(hint: It'll set the tone and fascinate him)
Tone down tattoos and piercings
(hint: Classic femininity will do)
Save some unique music or images on your phone
(hint: Inspire him)
Have a good appetite
(hint: No dieting. Enjoy your food – and life)

Tip: Avoid discussing gossip and negative news. He is attracted to positive and humorous women with sparkling personalities. But don't shine so bright that you command all of the attention.

CHAPTER 1

PREPARE YOURSELF

Catch his eye, capture his attention
Top 10 attention grabbers

1. Be assertive and take the initiative – without being bossy.
2. In conversation, approach a topic or everyday event from a new angle.
3. Be positive! Make sure your glass is half-full – or even better, just full.
4. Bring out the smile in your eyes and laughter in your voice.
5. Ask him out-of-the-ordinary questions.
6. Be playful. A childlike attitude will help him relax.
7. Be sparkling and fun.
8. Show your feelings, but don't get emotional.
9. Listen without prejudice.
10. Show off your feminine side and avoid anything aggressive.

The SHE. The woman!

The Pisces man seeks fun in his life. He wants to explore the world, and he treats every little thing as an adventure. But he also needs to feel safe and loved – and like a man. This means that his woman must be a little bit of everything: a fun companion, a sensitive, romantic and tender partner, a safe haven when life kicks his butt, and a hot lover. Seem unrealistic? Don't worry. Mr Pisces has the ability to bring out different sides of women, and it happens naturally.

The Essence of her
Feminine – romantic – sensitive – has a great sense of humour – strong– open-minded – has a upbeat voice – has smiling eyes – smart – alert – informed and willing to expand her mind – loves and explores life – introduces him to interesting experiences and people – attentive to his needs – takes the initiative – inspires him to explore life

---

Pisces arousal meter
From 0 to 100... In an hour or less, as long as the setting is right and he gets the encouragement he needs.

Remember: Be true to yourself

It doesn't matter if he is the most stunning guy you've ever met – if you don't match, you don't match. You may be able to put on a show for a while to hold his attention, but what's the point? We can't please everybody. We all have different needs, dreams, tastes and preferences. There's no such thing as a one-size-fits-all lover. Be yourself, and be true to who you are – always!

Very important: Never make him feel cornered. If you squeeze him too hard, he'll fly out of your hands like a bar of wet soap.

CHAPTER 2

THE FIRST DATE

Getting your foot in the door
The basics

Positive, laid back attitude! Greet him with a smile – a genuine one, not an 'I'm hot' smile. Be laid back about the date, as if you were going out with a friend.

Expose your mind. Make sure to have some interesting facts or topics up your sleeve – something that will make him pay attention. Surprise him with knowledge that is a little out of the ordinary.

Fun suggestions. There's no need to leave all the decisions about the date to him. Suggest something new and different.

Be cool, be playful. Drop him a few subtle hints, but don't be too obvious about your intentions – even if you're really into him.

Masculinity rocks. Although he likes strong women, he gets a kick out of someone who makes him feel like a Man. Show him that you truly enjoy being around him.

Listen with an open mind. Respect his opinions, even when you disagree. It doesn't hurt to be humorous about it.

Whatever you do...

- **DON'T** defend your principles for the sake of it.

- **DON'T** give the impression that you know best.

- **DON'T** be critical or negative.

- **DON'T** sport tattoos or piercings.

- **DON'T** wear outfits that are overly suggestive.

Remember,
If you feel the need to approach sensitive topics, make sure to be diplomatic

- **DON'T** keep looking at your watch or say you're worried about getting to bed too late.

- **DON'T** tell him to calm down or get a grip on reality.

- **DON'T** question his masculinity.

- **DON'T** be insensitive.

- **DON'T** flirt with other men.

about it! If he feels provoked and hurt, and he may turn his back on you.

Signs you're in - or not

Even if you've spent a nice, long evening together, it doesn't necessarily mean you're in – at least not romantically. He may find you interesting, fun and great company, but triggering his passion is something else entirely. This is what can make this guy such a challenge to figure out. Behaviours that would indicate serious interest from other men do not mean the same coming from him. His enthusiasm may simply signal that he thinks you're cool. However, there are some sure ways to know that you've hit a home run:

Chances are he will...

- make it clear that he'd like to see you again
- include you in future plans of things he'd like to do or try out
- prefer to talk to you even when he's surrounded by people
- seem genuinely interested in your views
- act enthusiastic when he's around you
- text to let you know you're on his mind

Not your type? Making an exit

Making an exit is easy, provided he doesn't have deep feelings for you – and this would be really odd. In his world, passion feeds on mutual interest; his flame cannot burn by itself. In any case, the quicker you make an exit, the better. Hanging around and pretending to be interested when you're not, hoping to spare his feelings, will make things a lot worse. The best approach is to be rational and polite about it. Let him know that you really enjoyed his company, but imply that you both might find greater happiness elsewhere.

If he has fallen deeply for you, you may need to divert his attention to your less attractive sides (feel free to produce a few fake ones). By making him see you in a different light, you'll show Mr Pisces that he was wrong about you all along – then he'll kick himself for being so stupid and take off.

Foolproof exit measures:

Sure, these are brutal – but they'll work. Be prepared to look like a bit of a jerk!

- Ridicule his sensitivity and question his masculinity
- Be rigid in your views, and toss in a few derogatory and discriminating remarks for good measure
- Forget to call or text him back
- Express your admiration for successful and ambitious men
- Tell him that men ought to focus more on exercising their biceps than their brains
- Respond to his suggestions with a yawn and a negative comment

CHAPTER 3

SEX'N STUFF

Seductive moves:
How to get him in the mood:

If he really likes you, getting him warmed up shouldn't be difficult at all. The fun thing about this guy is that he's up for sex at the weirdest times, in the weirdest places. He's not necessarily a kinky dude, but if the situation arises ... well, why miss out on a good experience?

Preferences and erotic nature

The Pisces man gets a kick out of being slowly undressed – preferably by a slightly dominant woman (even though she's just pretending). Don't rush it. This guy enjoys a good foreplay. It may start in an office chair, in the kitchen while making dinner, taking a shower after working out, or while getting ready to go out... Show a little initiative, and be gentle and firm. Dancing can lead to passionate activities – no matter where you are. Even playing footsies can be a fun place to start. The gentle brushing of bodies against each other can get him in the mood very quickly. If you've invited him over for a hot date, make sure to light some candles. Remember, this guy is attracted to sensual women, so be tender, seductive and a little sassy.

Hitting the right buttons

Although every sign has areas that are more sensitive than others, individual sensitivity may vary quite a bit. Don't go body-blind. Honing in on these erogenous zones and forgetting the rest of him is not a good idea. Use his erogenous zones to create sparks while turning him on, and as a passion booster when it gets heated. Watch his body language – including the most obvious of signs! Open your mind to the sensuality of touch and taste.

Key areas
Feet and ankles

Get it on
With a Pisces man, a casual foot massage can turn into something far spicier. Ankles, toes and soles of feet are particularly sensitive for men born under this sign. You'll have loads of opportunities to arouse him this way.

Arouse him
Kick off your shoe while having dinner and touch his ankles gently under the table. At home, complete the foot massage with gentle kisses around his ankles; brush your lips over his toes and the soles of his feet. Apply a little pressure to avoid tickling him. Even when you work your way up to sex, don't neglect his feet. Try positions that allow you to fondle and touch his feet. Let him explore you with his toes. You may be in for a pleasant surprise...

Surprise him

This man is a dreamer, and this carries over into his erotic life. Ask him about his fantasies and – as long as they're not too far out there – whether he would like to do more than just fantasise...

Spice it up

Rub his feet with warm oil. Let your hands slide around and between his toes, and round it off with gentle kisses.

Remember: This man is perceptive and picks up on hints easily. Be aware of how you come across, and don't send him mixed signals – he will notice all of them, and it will only confuse him.

His expectations

Be present! This man is no self-starter. It takes two to tango, especially when it comes to sex. If you seem reluctant or even a little ignorant, then you'll find he can't be bothered. There's no space in his bed for lazy partners.

Express pleasure. Besides wanting you to be active during sex, he also expects some sort of feedback. No, you don't have to be vocal about it. He's a good nonverbal communicator, too.

New ideas. Being assertive is a plus. Go ahead and expand his erotic horizons – he'll appreciate it. Remember, although he enjoys trying new things, anything too vulgar is a complete turn-off.

Bring it on! If you're passionate, liberated, impulsive and romantic, Mr Pisces will respond by transforming his boyish charm into hot, erotic masculinity.

Make it fun. A partner who can introduce him to new experiences will always make him happy.

Embrace his enthusiasm. Don't give him the 'look' if he suggests trying something unusual or having sex at the spur of the moment. This will hurt his feelings and probably turn him off you for quite some time.

Your sensual preferences
Quiz yourself and find out whether this man is for you.

Where on the scale are you?
1 = Don't agree | 3 = Sure | 5 = Agree!

1. Sensitivity is important to get maximum pleasure from sex.
One a scale for 1 to 5, you are : 1 - 2 - 3- 4 - 5

2. Sensuality ought to be experienced in the mind as well as the body.
One a scale for 1 to 5, you are : 1 - 2 - 3- 4 - 5

3. Playful impulsiveness can make sex feel more liberating and satisfying.
One a scale for 1 to 5, you are : 1 - 2 - 3- 4 - 5

4. Foreplay is the key to a wonderful sex life.
One a scale for 1 to 5, you are : 1 - 2 - 3- 4 - 5

Score 15–20: You may find yourself having sex often, simply because you manage to create the opportunities for it.
Score 10–14: You probably manage to communicate with your partner on many levels, which enables you to experience sex more deeply.
Score 5–9: Although there will be passion and fun between you, you may get a little confused about your partner's sensitivity. Don't think too much. Allow yourself to get carried away.
Score 1–4: His style may be a little sensitive, but he is open to suggestions. Communicate and guide him gently, and he may pump up the passion.

CHAPTER 4

GENERAL STUFF

The big picture

Keep in mind that the characteristics of a Pisces may vary quite a bit depending on where within the sign he was born, as well as a wide range of additional astrological factors. But for now, let's stick to the basics. Just remember: don't jump to conclusions as soon as you meet him. Give him room to shine. Get to know the man behind the sign.

His personality: Pros and cons

Pros
- Able to admit he was wrong
- Both masculine and sensitive
- Has an incredible memory
- Knowledgeable
- Empathetic
- Perceptive and understanding
- Positive and playful
- A romantic dreamer
- Easygoing
- Supportive and motivational
- Makes friends easily
- Seeks adventure
- Appreciates the beauty in life
- Enjoys style and quality

Cons
- Can get absorbed in himself
- Avoids difficult decisions
- Remembers negative things
- Absorbed his own interests
- Blunt and hurtful when upset
- Lives in his own world
- Avoids confrontation
- Argumentative when provoked
- Not particularly ambitious
- Indecisive; fails to commit
- Emotionally insecure
- Oversensitive
- Moody
- Overindulgent when stressed

Tip: How to show romantic interest

Appeal to his feelings. Pick up a book that means something to him, a bottle of wine you know he likes, or a little delicacy that tugs at his heartstrings. Anything personal will strike a chord with this man.

Romantic Vibes

Mr Pisces:
The romantic and adventurous partner

The essence

Hooked. As soon as he finds the woman, he won't let her go easily. Sweet messages, creative invitations, little gifts and an almost naïve openness are strong indications that Mr Pisces is hooked.

Romantic spotlight. When in love, he gives the woman centre stage in his life. Work, hobbies and friends are pushed down on his list of priorities – especially when the romance is new.

Going for it! He can be surprisingly assertive when he's made up his mind. Should you be so lucky to experience a Pisces in love, you'll find it very hard to say no.

Worth waiting for. Although he may wish you'd proclaim your love for him right away, he does realise that patience can be good, and sometimes even necessary. He will never pressure you, but he will give you subtle hints.

A true romantic. He will bring romance to your life from dawn to dusk – and even during the night, if you're awake.

Spoiling you. He'll call or text during the day to let you know he's thinking about you. He'll surprise you with breakfast in bed or buy a little something that he knows will mean a lot to you. In other words, he'll make life wonderful.

Tip: How to show erotic interest

Be playful about it – and direct, but not crude. Make your assertiveness feminine and flirty, and things will go to another level – provided you are in a setting that allows for it!

Erotic Vibrations

Mr Pisces:
The sensitive and playful lover

The essence

Surprise! The first time you encounter Mr Pisces in bed, you will probably be surprised. What happened to the sweet and gentle guy? Here, he'll transform into a passionate man who will take your breath away. Any trace of his shyness and insecurity will disappear.

No fiddling. Assertive, intense and hot ... this guy is a sensual dream who knows his way around women. There will be no nervous fiddling when he's around. This guy is no roaring Leo or fierce Scorpio. He's focused on the sensual sides to sex.

Expand your erotic mind. In his opinion, sex shouldn't be confined to the body; it should be a journey of the mind as well.

Dreams and fantasies. Some Pisces get a kick out of exploring erotic dreams and fantasies, but for most part, this man will prefer to have sex in nice, comfortable surroundings.

Impulsive. Sex is more than a once-a-week-on-a-Friday kind of thing for him. He is impulsive and may suggest sex at odd times (a sassy lunch break, etc.).

Just for kicks. Even though he is sexually assertive, he doesn't mind a dominant partner. Things can get steamy if a fully dressed woman asks him to take his clothes off!

CHAPTER 5

COMPATIBILITY QUIZ

Are you banging your head against the wall, or does he unleash your positive potential? Do you provoke him or bring out the best in him? Does he make you throw your arms up in exasperation, or do you feel inspired and complete in his company? Are the two of you headed towards doom or dream? Take the test to find out.

Question 1.
Are you able to see things from different perspectives?

A. Yes – it's important to avoid misunderstandings.
B. Mostly, provided I'm not angry or provoked.
C. Blah, blah, blah. I'm no shrink!

Question 2.
What do you do when your guy tells you about his dreams and everything he wants to achieve?

A. Listen, of course. However, I do take some of his ideas with a pinch of salt.
B. Yawn. My guy tends to live in his head. I prefer to focus on the real world.
C. I love a man with ideas. It inspires me and makes me more creative.

(cont.)

Question 3.
You're having a discussion, and it gets a little heated. What's your approach?

A. I always speak my mind, no matter what. If he can't take the heat, he should step away from the fire.
B. I try not to step on people's toes, but I tend to get passionate about topics that are important to me.
C. I feel we achieve more by listening and learning from each other. I'd try to keep the discussion from turning into an argument.

Question 4.
Do you participate actively when having sex?

A. Yes, of course. Sex is not just about receiving; it's about giving – and that can be a great turn-on in itself.
B. I'm not very assertive, and I prefer my partner to take the initiative.
C. It depends on my mood, really. Sometimes it's nice to be pampered; other times, I'm all over my partner.

Question 5.
How about erotic fantasies? Should they be kept secret, or…

A. The definition of a fantasy is something private and personal – and that's how they should stay!
B. Sharing fantasies with a man I trust can spice things up quite a bit…
C. I wouldn't mind talking about his fantasies, provided they're not too kinky. I may even share some of mine.

Question 6.
What kind of guy turns you on?

A. A romantic, caring type.
B. Someone who's sensual, intelligent and creative.
C. A masculine stud.

Question 7.
Do you believe there are guys who have genuine faith in the goodness of people?

A. I think so ... if not, the world would be a very cynical place.
B. The goodness of people? Sounds like something from the sixties. I want a real man – not a 'Peace, man!'
C. I think most people have an inherent sense of goodness – some guys more than others – and I like that.

Question 8.
You've been seeing this guy for a few weeks, and things are getting serious. How do you expect him to move the relationships forward?

A. Give me loads of freedom and leave it up to me to call him.
B. Spend as much time with me as possible.
C. Take the initiative, introduce me to his friends and suggest interesting things to do.

Question 9.
Do you find it easy to show your feelings?

A. I don't wear my heart on my sleeve, no. Why be vulnerable when I don't have to?
B. Sure. It's always good to talk about things – including feelings. It's the perfect way to establish trust.
C. I'm very sensitive, so emotions play a big part in my life.

Question 10.
You just met a guy, and the two of you hit it off. Would you prefer him to take it slow and ease into things, or are you eager to get to know him?

A. I definitely want to get to know him – fast!
B. Depends on the guy, really. If the chemistry is there, I don't mind things progressing naturally.
C. I'd prefer him to pull back a little. I never rush into things, even though it might be tempting at times.

SCORE	A	B	C
Question 1	10	5	1
Question 2	5	1	10
Question 3	1	10	5
Question 4	10	1	5
Question 5	1	10	5
Question 6	5	10	1
Question 7	5	1	10
Question 8	1	10	5
Question 9	1	5	10
Question 10	10	5	1

75 – 100
Once in a while, it just happens. The chemistry is there, love and romance grow quickly out of nowhere, and whatever seemed grey and boring in your life suddenly bursts with colour. This guy is like a magic wand ... and he probably has one, too. Should you ever have a moment of doubt about the relationship, call him. As soon as you hear his voice, your insecurities will disappear. You may not agree on everything, but this can actually be a good thing. It will allow you to explore each other's minds and widen your horizons. Enjoy!

51 – 74
If you let go, the two of you could get really into each other – and that's a pretty good start. So what if he doesn't aspire to become the next Mr Universe or spend hours at the gym, pumping his muscles? This is a good-looking guy with a relaxed attitude and a unique sensitivity. Sure, you may wish he could be more assertive at times. However, his energy, tenderness and consideration for others make up for his lack of high-flying ambition. This leaves a lot up to you. Why not make an effort to come up with some ideas and suggestions? Add a bit of adventure to a grey day. Not only will the two of you have fun together, but Mr Pisces will be even more hooked on you.

26 – 50

Have you started talking to yourself yet? Do you mumble under your breath when he loses track of time or forgets dates, shopping lists and appointments? Try to ignore the little hiccups. This man has got a 1000 things going on in his mind. Can you blame him for being absent-minded? Remember, he's a kid at heart. Nagging and criticising will yield nothing but bad vibes. He may even retreat into himself – and stay there until you can't take it anymore. There is one word you must remember: D-I-P-L-O-M-A-C-Y. If you fail on this, he'll fly out of your grip like a bar of soap that's been squeezed too hard. If you're looking for a super-masculine alpha male, you can forget Mr Pisces – he finds those guys pathetic, anyway. Don't try to turn him in to a muscular hunk, because you won't succeed. You'll have to either let him go or love him for who he is.

10 – 25

He may have been fun company at first, but how do you feel now? Is he holding you back? Does he lack the fierce energy you need to thrive? Are you becoming a little too independent for his sensitive nature? Do you crave a more ambitious guy who can get going without you kicking his butt? Love is wonderful; love is heavenly – but love requires a lot of work. Sometimes it's worth it and sometimes it's not You have to figure out whether this is love or temporary excitement – and if it's worth it, or if you and your Pisces stand a better chance seeking happiness elsewhere.

Thoughts…
He has his quirky sides which may charm you or annoy you - depending on your mood. Look beneath the surface.

...just a final note:
This book has not been approved by your date and should be treated accordingly. He or she *may* not agree with the content.

www.ingramcontent.com/pod-product-compliance
Lightning Source LLC
Chambersburg PA
CBHW071310150426
43191CB00007B/571